Thinking Through Second Corinthians

A Study Guide and Exposition

L. A. Mott, Jr.

SUNESIS PUBLISHING
Perry, Florida

Copyright © 2002 by L. A. Mott, Jr.
All rights reserved.

Published by **Sunesis Publishing Company**
424 S. McKinley Maddox Rd., Perry, Florida 32347
www.sunesispublishing.com

The Apostle Paul desired that disciples would receive "all riches of the full assurance of *understanding*, that they may know the mystery of God, even Christ, in whom are all the treasures of wisdom and knowledge hidden" (Colossians 2:1–3, ASV). The Greek word translated "understanding" is *sunesis*, and the mission of ***Sunesis Publishing*** is to provide resources which will assist disciples in their quest for these riches.

Publisher's Cataloging-in-Publication
(Provided by Quality Books, Inc.)

Mott, L. A.
   Thinking through Second Corinthians : a study guide and exposition / L.A. Mott, Jr. — 1st ed.
   p. cm. — (Thinking through the Bible series)
   LCCN: 2001098343
   ISBN: 0971648700

   1. Bible. N.T. Corinthians, 2nd—Study and teaching.
I. Title.

BS2675.5.M68 2002   227'.3'0071
                                     QBIOI-201501

Printed in Canada

TABLE OF CONTENTS

Preface to *Thinking Through Second Corinthians* 7

Part One: Discussion of Apostolic Ministry, Interwoven with Narrative of Paul's Relations with the Corinthians
Second Corinthians 1–7

Lesson 1 (Brief Introduction and 1:1–14) 11
Lesson 2 (1:15–2:11) 17
Lesson 3 (2:12–3:18) 24

Appendix: The Letter and the Spirit 35

Lesson 4 (4:1–5:10) 39
Lesson 5 (5:11–6:10) 51
Lesson 6 (6:11–7:4) 61
Lesson 7 (7:5–16) 65

Part Two: The Collection for the Saints
Second Corinthians 8–9

Lesson 8 (ch. 8) 73
Lesson 9 (ch. 9) 80

Part Three: Vindication of Paul's Apostleship Against False Teachers
Second Corinthians 10–13

Lesson 10 (ch. 10) 89
Lesson 11 (ch. 11) 101
Lesson 12 (12:1–13) 115
Lesson 13 (12:14–13:14) 120

Abbreviations

AG:	Arndt & Gingrich, *Greek-English Lexicon*
ASV:	*American Standard Version of the Bible*
EDNT:	*Exegetical Dictionary of the New Testament*
EGT:	*Expositor's Greek Testament*
Grk:	Greek
GT:	Grimm-Thayer, *Greek-English Lexicon*
KJV:	*King James Version of the Bible*
NEB:	*New English Bible*
NASB:	*New American Standard Bible*
NIV:	*New International Version*
NKJ:	*New King James Version*
NT:	New Testament
OT:	Old Testament
RSV:	*Revised Standard Version*
TDNT:	*Theological Dictionary of the New Testament*
Trench:	R. C. Trench, *Synonyms of the New Testament*
VED:	W. E. Vine, *Expository Dictionary of the New Testament*

Preface to *Thinking Through Second Corinthians*

This study guide is a complete revision and enlargement of the original from the early eighties. Like the other revisions, it is more than a study guide, in many ways having the character of a brief commentary. I am anxious to get Bible students, especially preachers and teachers, into Second Corinthians because it has been such a blessing to me. Four times in two years I have taken groups through this epistle. It never gets old. Each time I have felt its power again, and been moved and better equipped to do the work of the gospel in our times. I have also been delighted to see eager students share my joy in this epistle, and to be touched and deeply moved by its power.

Nowhere in his writings has Paul opened his heart to a greater extent. He had seen the church he had planted, converts whom he regarded as his own spiritual children, invaded by teachers of a different gospel in an attempt to undermine and discredit him and to take this church away from him. It is amazing that the church would listen and tolerate such invaders in their midst instead of speaking up for Paul and sending them on their way. But they did not. So Paul must explain his ministry and defend himself. The truth of the gospel and the salvation of this church was at stake. So Paul pours himself into the effort, making a full exposition of the apostolic ministry and of his motives and methods. In the process his readers see into his heart as never before.

What a wonderful opportunity we have to understand gospel ministry and to get before us such a wonderful model to imitate as we serve the Lord Christ today. We cannot be apostles, but we must by all means endeavor to have the heart of an apostle as we do the work of Christ today.

A brief explanation with regard to the schedule is necessary. I have divided Second Corinthians into thirteen lessons to suggest how it may be naturally fitted into a program that operates strictly on a quarterly basis. And the lessons can be done on a thirteen lesson schedule. But as an experienced teacher I would probably want to divide certain lessons into two, and go deep enough to try to get my students really to feel the power of the Word. So I was tempted to offer some suggestions about dividing these lessons into Parts A & B. But inexperienced teachers would probably not know what to do with the extra time, and experienced teachers will probably not need my suggestions. So I decided to leave well enough alone. And I would caution any teacher against dragging a study out too long. I find that many teachers who think they are going "deep" have actually drifted away from the text. One cannot tell whether they are studying Second Corinthians or Proverbs. Better to move right on through the text, doing what you can in the allotted time, and looking forward to the day when you can return to Second Corinthians as a more experienced teacher. As a young teacher I often reached the end of a course of study thinking: My! Now I am ready to begin. Alas! My students were ready for something else. So I would encourage young teachers to move rapidly through the Bible, but with hope of returning to each book at a later time when you have more to bring to it.

Quite a few students and teachers have made use of my recorded lectures in preparation for classes, or for their own edification. The cassettes multiply the study time available to busy people. They can be used while travelling, jogging, waiting for appointments, doing the dishes, and what not. The lecture series on Second Corinthians embodies my most mature thinking. Done in late 1999, it runs to about 13 hours. Some of you may want to complement your use of the book by adding these tapes.

As with some of my other books, this one has been published with the help of many "partners"—people who made an advance commitment to buy at least one copy. Each of these "partners" has become, in effect, a co-publisher. I feel indebted to each. But one partner has done more than any other to make this particular book a reality. My son Rick, who has always encouraged my work, has invested countless hours in the production of *Thinking Through Second Corinthians.* He designed the cover, did the final composition work, making the book more stylish, has become the book's publisher, and altogether, has rescued my faltering publishing operation and produced a better book than this one would otherwise have been. I take pleasure in recognizing folk who have been special partners in my teaching and publishing efforts, and Rick has meant so much to this book that nothing could be more fitting than to inscribe it ...

> To An Extraordinary Partner
> My Son, Richard Hailey Mott,
> inscribed with love, appreciation
> and admiration

PART ONE

*Discussion
of Apostolic Ministry,
Interwoven with Narrative
of Paul's Relations
with the Corinthians*

SECOND CORINTHIANS 1-7

LESSON 1
Second Corinthians 1:1–14

Brief Introduction to Second Corinthians

Occasion and Purpose

Second Corinthians was written about a year after the first Corinthian epistle (2 Cor. 8:10; 9:1f). To date it in the mid-fifties is sufficient for our purposes. It was written from Macedonia (2 Cor. 2:12f; 7:5–7; 8:1; 9:1–5) after Paul's Ephesian ministry (Acts 20:1). Paul was planning to come to Corinth on his way to Jerusalem (Acts 19: 21f; 20:1f; 2 Cor. 12:14a; 13:1). The letter, apparently carried by Titus, aims at moving the Corinthians to be ready for Paul's coming (8:6; 9:1–5; 10:1–6; 12:19–21; 13:1–10).

After Paul sent the extremely critical first Corinthian epistle his Corinthian "children" (6:13; 12:14) remained heavy on his heart. He was anxious to know how they had taken his reproof (2 Cor. 1–7, especially 1:23–2:13 & 7:5–7). He had sent Titus to Corinth, either bearing the first letter or soon afterwards, and his heart was burdened as he anxiously awaited the arrival of Titus from Corinth with a report (2 Cor. 2:12f; 7:5–7). Second Corinthians was evidently written soon after Titus rejoined Paul in Macedonia. The arrival of Titus with good news from Corinth greatly relieved Paul's anxiety, but not entirely. The response to Paul's letter was everything Paul hoped for (2 Cor. 7:5–16). But still the state of the church gave reason for concern.

Another problem had come to Corinth in the form of false teachers, Jews (11:22), evidently teaching some form of Judaism. Perhaps the problem was not altogether new (for cf. 1 Cor. 9:1), but had become more serious. These teachers had attacked Paul, trying to undermine and discredit his apostleship and so to steal this church which Paul had labored to plant, which was so dear to his heart (2:4; 6:11–13; 7:2f; 12:15), and to bring it under their influence.

As we shall see, Paul expresses great confidence in his Corinthians. On the other hand, they had not stood up for Paul as they should have (12:11). Some seemed to be listening to the charges against Paul. Yet this church had been founded by Paul and the Corinthians were his own "children." Paul's heart must have been breaking. But it was not just a personal matter. It was not just Paul's reputation and personal standing that were at stake. It was the truth of the gospel, and the salvation of the Corinthian disciples that hung in the balance. Unwilling to write them off, Paul comes to their rescue in this epistle. He had to defend himself or see the message resting upon his apostolic authority swept away.

In no other epistle does Paul bare his heart so fully as in this one. No other epistle takes us so deep into the great heart of the apostle. What a treasure God has preserved in this epistle for those who endeavor to do the work of the gospel today. We cannot be apostles, but we must most earnestly endeavor to have the heart of an apostle. We must turn to Second Corinthians again and again in order to understand the ministry of the gospel, the motives and method of the apostle, and to find inspiration, motivation and power for our own work in the twenty-first century.

Three Parts

Of three clear-cut divisions in the epistle, Part One consists of Second Corinthians 1–7. It is structured around a narrative of Paul's relations with the Corinthians, a kind of update of Paul's affairs after the first epistle as related to the Corinthians.[1] But interwoven with this narrative is a full discussion of Paul's apostolic ministry. Hence the heading of Part One: *Discussion of Apostolic Ministry, Interwoven with Narrative of Paul's Relations with the Corinthians*.

The subject of Part Two (chs. 8–9) is *The Collection for the Saints*. The Corinthians seemed to be lagging behind with regard to the order Paul had given in First Corinthians 16:1–2, perhaps under the influence of Paul's critics in Corinth. This section encourages them to complete the job they had started a year before. It deals with preparations that needed to be made in advance of Paul's coming. See especially 8:6 and 9:1–5.

Part Three (chs. 10–13) is *A Vindication of Paul's Apostleship Against the Attack of False Teachers*. As we shall see, this section too aims at getting the Corinthians ready for Paul's coming. See e. g. 12:19–21.

Thus each part is written with Paul's anticipated visit to Corinth in view. Paul had delayed his coming (1:15–2:4) in order to give the Corinthians plenty of opportunity to correct the things that were amiss. And this entire letter is aimed at moving them to get ready for Paul's coming. He did not want to come to them "with a rod," but "in love and a spirit of gentleness" (1 Cor. 4:21; cf. 2 Cor. 1:23–2:1; 9:1–5; 10:1–6; 12:19–13:10).

---

[1] For this structure, pay particular attention to 1:15–2:13 and 7:5–16.

Salutation (1:1–2)

The three main points of the salutation can be brought out with questions:

1a. What is the capacity in which Paul addresses the Corinthians?

1b. Discuss the significance of the phrase *through the will of God* in view of the effort that was being made in Corinth to discredit Paul's apostleship.

2a. How does Paul address the Corinthians?

2b. Some make much of Paul's addressing the Corinthian saints as a church of God (here and 1 Cor. 1:1f) in spite of all that was wrong with it. But would it have been a church of God if it had rejected the counsel of one who wrote with the authority of an apostle of Christ Jesus? (cf. 2:9).

3. How does Paul greet the Corinthians?

Partners in Affliction and in Comfort: Paul and the Corinthians (1:3–11)

Consider whether this heading captures the essence of this passage, also the significance of the passage in view of the effort of false teachers to drive a wedge between Paul and the Corinthians (see esp. chs. 10–13). Then notice the link with the next passage (12–14).

Outburst of Praise (3–5)

1. If you will read the first seven chapters, taking special note of what is said about Paul's relations with the Corinthians (cf. esp. 1:23–2:4, 2:12f & 7:5–16), you will understand why this epistle begins as it does. What accounts for the outburst of emotion with which the epistle begins?

2. God could be characterized in many ways, of course (cf. 1 Cor. 1:9; 10:13; Eph. 1:17; etc.). How is he characterized in this exclamation of praise, and why?

3. How did God comfort Paul, according to 7:5–7?

4. What divine purpose would be served by the comfort extended to Paul by God? (4).

5. Make use of Colossians 1:24 and First Peter 4:12–16 to explain "the sufferings of Christ" (5).

LESSON 1

Divine Purpose of Affliction and Comfort (6–7)

1. Paul points out that both the affliction and the comfort experienced by him (and his colleagues) is for the sake of the Corinthians. How would that be true with regard to the afflictions (6a)? (cf. 4:7–15).

2. How then would the comfort ministered to them work for the benefit of the Corinthians? (6b).

3. What made Paul's hope for the Corinthians steadfast or firm? (7).

An Illustration of the Divine Comfort (8–11)

Affliction in Asia (8f)

The particulars are not explained. But Acts 19:23–41 certainly illustrates the potential for danger in Asia. Five descriptive expressions are piled one on the other to characterize the affliction experienced in Asia. Summarize by answering the question: How bad was it?

Divine Purpose (9)

1. The details of the situation are not important. The divine purpose is. Why did God permit Paul to be brought so low?

2. What in the situation would serve that purpose?

3. What encouragement can this passage be in times of affliction?

Deliverance and the Hope of Deliverance (10)

1. In the desperate circumstances (8–9), nothing was left for Paul and his coworkers but to trust "in God who raises the dead." What was the outcome?

2. What in verse 10 indicates that God's purpose in these circumstances (9) was realized and that they had learned the lesson God wanted to teach them?[2]

---

[2] Paul knew the experience in Asia was not the end of his afflictions. When this letter was written from Macedonia he knew trouble awaited in Jerusalem. Soon after, he wrote to the Roman Christians from Achaia, asking them to "strive together with me in your prayers to God for me; that I may be delivered from them that are disobedient in Judea" (Rom. 15: 30f). As he left Achaia a Jewish plot forced a change in his travel plans (Acts 20:3). Soon after, he told the Ephesian elders at Miletus that the Holy Spirit was warning him in every city that "bonds and afflictions"

Note continued on next page

Corinthian Help (11)

1. In what way were the Corinthian Christians expected to help Paul?
2. What else were they expected to do?
3. What attitude toward the Corinthians is implied in verse 11?[3]

Ground of Paul's Expectation:
The Sincerity of his Conduct (1:12–14)

These verses are a transition passage. They relate to the preceding verse as supplying a reason for Paul's expectation that the Corinthians would petition God on his behalf and then give thanks for his deliverance. That expectation is founded upon the conscious sincerity of his behavior toward them.

But the short passage also leads up to the defense of his integrity against the charge of fickleness in the following verses.

General Integrity (12)

Greek *kauchesis* (glorying) refers to the act of glorying or boasting; in other words, a claim Paul can make. What claim could he make, which gave reason for his expectation that the Corinthians would be supportive of him (as in 11)?[4]

---

remained for him (Acts 20:23). All along the way to Jerusalem he was warned of danger awaiting him (Acts 21:4, 10–14). But God had delivered him before and he had hope "that he will also still deliver us." Sometimes God delivers from death, as in Asia; sometimes he delivers through death (2 Tim. 4:18 with 6–8). But he always delivers those who trust him.

[3] Paul expected them to support him in his trials by prayer for his deliverance [as he made request of the Romans (Rom. 15:30f)], and then send up thanks to God once he was delivered. They would be his partners both in affliction and in comfort. This expectation represents strong confidence in their attitude toward him, despite the efforts of false teachers to take this church from him.

[4] Such boasting is not bad. Paul is making a claim that any preacher needs to be able to make. One cannot serve the Lord effectively without being able to make this claim with regard to integrity.

In the grace of God stands in contrast to *in fleshly wisdom*. Grace is more than the quality in God by which sins are forgiven and salvation provided. It also provides gifts for ministry. Consult such passages as Romans 12:3, First Cor. 1:4–7; 3:10; 15:10; Eph. 3:7, 8 for the usage here.

Special Application to his Letters (13)
Consider what Paul means when his claim to general integrity (in 12) is specially applied to his writing (in 13a). Do people sometimes say or write one thing when they mean another, perhaps with some sort of hidden meaning?[5]

Paul's Hope with Regard to the Corinthians (14)
What hope does Paul hold with regard to the Corinthians?[6]

---

[5] Compare the charge against Paul, to which he responds in 15ff.

[6] *That we are your glorying*, i. e. men to boast about rather than to disown. The whole presentation here is more understandable when we realize that Paul had enemies in Corinth, who were out to undermine and discredit him and to take this church from him. See 3:1; 5:12; 10:1, 10; 11:12f; 12:11–18 for evidence.

Even as you also are ours. It was no one way street. They were his boast (cf. Phil. 4:1; 1 Thess. 2:19f), and he wanted them to feel the same toward him.

LESSON 2
Second Corinthians 1:15–2:11

EXPLANATION OF RECENT CONDUCT
SECOND COR. 1:15–2:11

The defense of Paul's integrity continues. A change of plans, even though made out of consideration for the Corinthians (cf. 1:23), was the occasion for an attack on Paul's integrity. The questions raised in 1:17 must be understood in the light of the presence of the false teachers in Corinth, who were trying to discredit Paul. See 3:1; 5:12; 10:1, 10; 11:12; 12:11–18 for their accusations.

The change of plans was used as evidence of a general lack of character. Paul first deals generally with the attack on his character, then explains the change of plans.

More was at stake here than a personal offense against Paul. The message Paul had preached was at stake. For that reason it was extremely important for Paul to defend his character. We must learn the vital lesson that the messenger must be a person of integrity. Otherwise opponents of the gospel will take hold of the weaknesses of the messenger in order to discredit the message.

The Defense of Paul's Integrity (1:15–22)

Paul's original plan (15–16) might have been communicated to the Corinthians either in a former, now lost letter (cf. 1 Cor. 5:9–11), during a visit to Corinth (2 Cor. 2:1; 12:14; 13:1), or by a messenger. He had planned to come first to Corinth; then to Macedonia; and then back to Corinth and on to Judea. But by the time he wrote First Corinthians he had decided to delay his coming to Corinth; to go first to Macedonia; and then to come to Corinth for a longer visit (1 Cor. 16:5–7). The change amounted to nothing, and friends would think nothing of it. But Paul had opponents in Corinth, who tried to represent this change of plan as indicative of a major character flaw.

Connection With Preceding Section

Go back to 1:12–14. Summarize Paul's testimony about himself with regard to both his behavior (12) and his writing (13), and relate this beginning to the overall explanation he makes in this section.

LESSON 2

The Change of Plan (15–16)

1. Draw upon verses 13-14 to explain what is meant by "in this confidence" (15).

2. Explain the change of plan indicated in verses 15-16 (cf. 1 Cor. 16:5–7).

3. Consider what is meant by "a second benefit (or grace)" (15).[1]

4. The idea of being "set forward" on one's journey (16; cf. 1 Cor. 16:6, 11) is brought out most clearly in Titus 3:13 & Third John 6 (in context). But see also Acts 15:3, 17:14f & Romans 15:24.

Questions Raised With Regard to Character (17)

1. What questions, growing out of this change of plan, does Paul raise about his character?[2]

2. What is implied by "the yea yea and the nay nay" (evidently meaning an emphatic yes and an equally emphatic no, both at the same time)?

Defense of Paul's Integrity Grounded on the Faithfulness of God (18–20)

1. What did Paul want the Corinthians to understand about his change of plan? (18).

2. How does God's faithfulness relate to the case? (18).[3]

3. Paul's denial (in 18) is supported by a statement concerning the One preached among the Corinthians by him and his companions (19).[4] How

---

[1] Every apostolic visit would aim at a communication of God's grace (cf. Rom. 1:11f). *Second* refers to the double visit. Otherwise, why this clause? If the allusion is to his original visit to Corinth, the clause would seem to be pointless. For even with the change of plans he did still intend to come to Corinth and that would certainly involve a communication of grace. Consider also that he had already visited Corinth a second time (cf. 2:1; 12:14; 13:1).

[2] Surely because these questions had been raised by critics in Corinth. Paul raises the questions in order to deal with them.

[3] *As* is a supplied word. A more literal translation would be: *But God is faithful*, or perhaps: *But God being faithful*. Recall Paul's description of his apostleship: "an apostle of Christ Jesus through the will of God" (1). Paul was an apostle because God willed it. It is incredible that God should have sent as his spokesman a man who was unreliable.

[4] Cf. Acts 18:5 for Silvanus (= Silas) and Timothy.

does this assertion concerning the One preached among them lend support to Paul's denial that his word was unreliable, vacillating, yea and nay at the same time?[5]

4a. Paul explains his statement *but in him is yea* (19) in verse 20. What is meant by that statement in light of Paul's explanation?

4b. Explain the promises of God in light of such references as Romans 1:2, 15:8 & Galatians 3:16.

4c. In what way does the proclamation of the Christ as the affirmation and fulfillment of the promises of God bring glory to God? (cf. Rom. 15:7f).[6]

The Integrity and Stability of Paul and Associates Underwritten by God Himself (21–22)

1. Clearly these two verses must be understood in their connection as bringing to a conclusion Paul's defense of his integrity and stability against the charge of lightness, fickleness and instability. How do these verses relate to the case Paul is making?[7]

2. How did Paul and his associates get the firmness and stability he claims?

---

[5] Would God send messengers whose word was unreliable to proclaim One who was such a solid affirmation of his own promises? This connection between the messenger and the message explains why the preachers of the Christ must be men of integrity. The opponents of the gospel will try to undermine the message by discrediting the messenger. More was at stake in Paul's defense of his integrity than just himself. The message itself was at stake.

[6] Take note also of *through us*—the ones through whom Christ was proclaimed as the fulfillment of God's promises (19). The fulfillment of God's promises in Christ was unto the glory of God through us. Think how much is given up when the integrity of these messengers is called in question. Certainly much more than the reputation of weak men, the very glory of God is at stake.

[7] It is important to pay attention to the context, in which the integrity of Paul is being defended against attack. These verses ascribe the stability of Paul's apostleship to the work of God himself. To attack Paul is to go against the work of God in him.

Consider the language:
Grk for "establishes" is *bebaioo*: "to make firm, establish, confirm, make sure" (GT, 99b). The present tense of the participle refers to a continuing act.

Note continued on next page

LESSON 2

The Reason for Paul's Change of Plan (1:23–2:4)

Having vindicated himself from the accusation of general "lightness" or "fickleness" (1:15–22), Paul now comes to the specific matter on which that accusation was based. He explains the real reason for his change of plan and delay in coming to Corinth. It was not due to fleshly or selfish motives, but out of consideration for the Corinthian disciples.

Reason as Concerns the Corinthians (1:23–24)

1. Paul's change of plan was not due to some flaw in his character (1:15–18). What was his reason? (1:23).[8]

2. Paul anticipates that his explanation of the delay in his coming might be misconstrued. What further explanation (24) guards against a misunderstanding of what he had written?[9]

Paul and his companions were also anointed with the Holy Spirit as was Jesus (Luke 4:18; Acts 10:38). This language indicates an inauguration to office in the manner of prophets (1 Kings 19:16; cf. Is. 61:1), priests (Ex. 28:37; 40:15; Lev. 6:22; Num. 35:25) and kings (1 Sam. 9:16; 10:1; 15:1; 16:3, 13) in ancient days.

God *also sealed us*, writes Paul. Grk *sphragizo* is "to set a seal upon, mark with a seal, to seal" (GT, 609), here (as in John 6:27) referring to an authenticating seal (cf. 12:12). Finally he *gave us the earnest of the Spirit in our hearts*. An earnest (Grk *arrabon*) is "money which in purchases is given as a pledge that the full amount will subsequently be paid" (GT, 75a). *In our hearts* points to the inspiration of the apostles (cf. 4:6), fully equipping them for their task.

[8] Observe how this explanation connects with First Cor. 4:21. Notice also the strength of Paul's assertion in this verse. *But I call God for a witness upon my soul*, so that "if he is lying, he will forfeit his salvation" (AG on *psuche*, 893b). He stakes the salvation or ruin of his soul upon it (Meyer).

[9] *To spare you* as an explanation of his delay in coming "might have suggested that he was a lord graciously sparing his subjects. He guards against this misconception. ... The Corinthian Christians have their own relationship to Christ; they themselves stand in faith, and it is Paul's task to be a fellow-helper of their joy" (Foerster in TDNT, III, 1097). The Greek *kurieuo* is "be lord or master,

Note continued on next page

Reason as Concerns Himself (2:1–2)

1. What determination had Paul formed about his coming to Corinth? (1).[10]

2. What reason does he give for this determination? (2).

Action Taken Consistent With This Determination: Purpose of First Corinthians (2:3–4)

1. What reason did Paul have for his previous letter, consistent with the determination he had formed (1)? (3a).

2. What confidence moved him to write with this stated purpose? (3b).

3. Describe Paul's feelings as he wrote the former letter (4a).

4. What was his aim in writing? (4b).

Closing the Case by Restoring the Sinner (2:5–11)

Having made reference to the first epistle, Paul now alludes to the flagrant and notorious case of incest which had been tolerated by the church (1 Cor. 5). The radical action called for in the case had not been intended to destroy the man or to get rid of him, but to save him (1 Cor. 5:5). The Corinthians had dealt forthrightly with the case, and their strong action had brought the man to repentance. But then they were slow to restore one who had sinned so grievously, even though he was deeply sorrowful and fully penitent.

---

rule, lord it (over), control" (AG, 458b). Paul's authority as an apostle was not absolute, but delegated; it was exercised only so far as he spoke for the one Lord to whom each Christian was solely responsible (cf. Rom. 14:4). Instead of exercising lordship over their faith, Paul adds, *we are helpers of your joy*, meaning "it is our business to be helpful to you, so that you rejoice" (Meyer), referring to the joy that would be theirs when they were pleasing to the one Lord and Master, Jesus Christ. The sentence uses a dative of respect: *for with respect to the faith you stand fast*. Recall the exhortation at First Cor. 16:13.

[10] He did not want to *come again in sorrow*, as would have been the case had he come with a rod to deal with impenitence (1 Cor. 4:21). Had Paul kept to his original plan (1:15f) he could not be sure his coming would not have been "in sorrow," as a previous visit had been. The previous sorrowful visit must have been during the Ephesian ministry, for his original plan had already been changed at the writing of First Corinthians (16:5–7). The upcoming visit would be the third trip to Corinth (12:14; 13:1).

LESSON 2

Paul's Concern for the Penitent Sinner (5–8)

1. Paul did not want to come to Corinth "in sorrow" (1). His intention in the first letter was "not that you should be made sorry" (4). But one man had caused sorrow (5), once First Corinthians 5 had brought conviction to the heart of the church. Explain the background of verse 5 in light of First Cor. 5.[11]

2. Paul's direction (in 1 Cor. 5) had been followed and had the desired effect. But now what was the problem? (6–7).

3. What was Paul afraid would be the effect, if the man was not forgiven and encouraged by the church? (7).[12]

4. What does he urge the church to do to prevent such an outcome? (8).[13]

---

[11] Some details of verse 5 need explanation. Paul would have been sorrowful, of course, at any such sinful condition. But perhaps he means he was not personally offended; he was not the injured party in the case. *But in part* (Grk *apo merous*) is explained in the lexicons to mean "in some degree" (AG, 506a), "in a measure, to some degree" (GT, 401a), as in Romans 15:24. The parenthetical remark *that I press not too heavily*, i. e., that I do not put too heavy a burden, explaining why he says *in part*, seems to refer to the burden Paul's language would put upon the now penitent sinner. See Meyer and Lenski.

[12] "The sadness (conceived as a hostile animal) is what swallows up. The context gives nothing more precise than the notion: *to be brought* by the sadness *to despair*, to the abandoning of all hope and of all striving after the Christian salvation" (Meyer).

[13] Grk *kuroo* is common in legal documents with the meaning "confirm, ratify, validate" (AG, 461a). The congregation had decided on action to be taken with reference to the man while he was in sin (1 Cor. 5:3–5; 2 Cor. 2:6). "The congregation has now to make another decision in the case of the man whom it has punished and who now sincerely repents of his fault (2 Cor. 2:7). Paul desires a decision whose content is love" (TDNT, III, 1098f). AG says the meaning is "decide in favor of love for someone" (461a); GT: "to make a public decision that love be shown to a transgressor by granting him pardon" (366b). Meyer explains: "to resolve in reference to him love—i. e. through a resolution of the church to determine regarding him, that he be regarded and treated as an object of Christian brotherly love."

Motive for Confirming Love Toward the Penitent Sinner Founded Upon Paul's Aim in the First Letter (9–11)

1. What aim did Paul have (in addition to that indicated in 3f) in writing the previous letter? (9).[14]

2. The church had been obedient to Paul's initial direction (1 Cor. 5). But now they must obey further by forgiving the sinner. Of what does Paul assure them in verse 10?

3. What purpose for extending forgiveness to the sinner is indicated in verse 11?[15]

---

[14] This purpose should be considered by those who draw attention to Corinth's status as a "church of God" (1 Cor. 1:2) in spite of having so much wrong with it. What if this church had brushed aside the epistle from "an apostle of Jesus Christ through the will of God"? What kind of church would it then have been?

[15] Greek *noema*, "the result of the activity of the mind" (TDNT, IV, 961f), here refers to Satan's evil thoughts, plans, plots, purposes or designs (AG, 540b; cf. GT, 427). This incident is a good illustration of the diversity of Satan's evil schemes. He seduces a disciple into sin, with its evil consequences not only for him but for the church too (1 Cor. 5). But he does not quit even when that sin has been dealt with in a forthright manner. He can still gain the upper hand if forgiveness is not forthcoming after discipline has produced repentance, gaining the sinner after all when he is overwhelmed by despair, and perhaps disrupting the unity of a church unable to agree on the appropriate action to take.

LESSON 3
Second Corinthians 2:12–3:18

MINISTERS OF A NEW COVENANT
SECOND COR. 2:12–3:18

Narrative Resumed: From Troas to Macedonia (2:12–13)

Paul continues the narrative of his movements as related to the Corinthians. He has summarized his original plan to come first to Corinth, then to Macedonia, then back to Corinth and on to Judea (1:15f). He has acknowledged that the itinerary he gave them in First Corinthians 16:5–7, the plan to go first to Macedonia and then to Corinth for a longer stay, represented a change of plan; but he explained the reason for the delay in coming to Corinth (1:23–2:4). The movements summarized here accord with the revised plan given in First Corinthians. Thus the discussion of Paul's apostolic ministry is interwoven with a narrative of his relations with the Corinthians.

1. Relate the movements described here to Luke's record in Acts (20:1).[1]

2. Using the immediate context (1:23–2:4) and the related passage at 7:5ff where Paul resumes the thread of thought, explain the feelings described here.

3. Why did Paul's anxiety remain unrelieved at Troas?[2]

---

[1] From Troas Paul went to Macedonia, retracing the ground covered on his first trip to Macedonia (Acts 16:8–12). The present movements fit into Luke's narrative at Acts 20:1. The stop at Troas is not the one mentioned in Acts 20:5f, for at that time he was not headed toward Macedonia but Judea. Perhaps the open door mentioned here explains why Paul made another stop at Troas on his way to Judea after stops at Macedonia and Achaia.

[2] *No relief for my spirit* alludes to the anxiety Paul felt in writing First Corinthians (2:3f), and then afterwards due to the uncertainty with regard to how the letter had been received. Titus had been sent to Corinth either with the letter or soon afterwards (cf. 7:5–16). He was expected to come through Macedonia from Corinth, and then to continue on to Troas. Traveling over the same route in the opposite direction Paul

Note continued on bottom of next page

Thanksgiving for the Triumphal Progress of the Gospel (2:14–17)

1. What unrecorded (at this point) event explains this sudden exclamation of thanksgiving? (cf. 7:5–16 with 2:12–13).

2. Summarize the characterization of God, which moves Paul to praise him (14).[3]

3. What is the imagery by which the role of Paul and his colleagues is illustrated in the last clause of verse 14?[4]

4. The imagery continues in 15f, but with a slight change. In what way?

---

would meet him somewhere and get news about Corinth. He thought Titus might reach Troas and join him there. But it was not to be, and the news that would have relieved Paul's anxiety was delayed. With no relief for his spirit Paul left the open door in Troas and went on to Macedonia.

[3] The Greek verb *triambeuo* seems never to have the causative sense: "cause to triumph" (KJV). GT, 292a and AG, 363 do allow this meaning, but without citing evidence. The meaning is rather: to lead in triumph, i. e. in a triumphal procession such as was used to celebrate the victories of a Roman emperor. But the objects of the leading are not the victors who share the triumph, but the captives who have been overcome. Paul himself had once fought against God, but had been taken captive by him. Paul and his colleagues were now led about as slaves of the victorious God. In Christ Paul has become "one of the captives by means of whom the knowledge and fame of the victory is made manifest. He rejoices that he has been so used by God, as would appear from the tidings which Titus has brought him" (Bernard in EGT). Meyer translates: "*who always triumphs over us* (apostolic teachers)—i. e. *who does not cease to represent us as his vanquished before all the world*, as a triumpher celebrates his victories. In this figurative aspect Paul considers himself and his like as conquered by God through their conversion to Christ. And after this victory of God his triumph now consists in all that those conquered by their conversion effect as servants and instruments of God for the Messianic kingdom in the world; it is by the results of apostolic activity that God continually, as if in triumph, shows himself to the eyes of all as the victor, to whom His conquered are subject and serviceable. For the concrete instance before us, this perpetual triumph of God exhibited itself in the happy result which He wrought in Corinth through the apostle's letter (as Paul learned in Macedonia through Titus, 7:6)." For further discussion consult J. B. Lightfoot on Colossians 2:15 and TDNT, III, 160.

[4] The idea of a savor also alludes to the Roman triumphal procession, the savor coming from the flowers and incense which perfumed the air.

LESSON 3

5. Explain the crucial issues, the stakes, involved in the preaching of the gospel (15f). What difference does it make whether one accepts the gospel?[5]

6. What gives rise to the question at the end of 16?[6]

7. The question is supported by reference to the contrast between the apostolic company and most teachers (17). What characteristics of a faithful teacher are set forth in verse 17?[7]

---

[5] In the Roman triumphal processions the incense had the smell of victory for the victors, but the smell of slavery or death for prisoners of war.

[6] It is a question with regard to competence for such awesome responsibility. *Who* implies: Hardly anyone (as in Is. 53:1). Yet 14–16a implies that Paul and his associates have somehow been made adequate for the task. So the question is: Who, besides us few? This implication of the question is supported by the contrast between the apostolic company and most teachers (in 17).

[7] Grk *kapeleuo* occurs only here in the NT. Nearly all the later translations (e. g., ASV margin, NASB, NKJ, RSV, NEB, NIV) render the clause in which it appears along the lines of *peddling the word of God*—not merely corrupting (KJV) or adulterating the word of God, but doing so for profit. The synonym in 4:2 (Grk *doloo*) means corrupting or adulterating, but does not in itself include the idea of doing so for gain. "The meanings are not identical. While both involve the deceitful dealing of adulterating the word of truth, *kapeleuo* has the broader significance of doing so in order to make dishonest gain. Those to whom the apostle refers in 2:17 are such as make merchandise of souls through covetousness (cf. Titus 1: 11; 2 Pet. 2:3, 14–15; Jude 11, 16; Ezek. 13:19); accordingly 'hucksterizing' would be the most appropriate rendering in this passage, while 'handling deceitfully' is the right meaning in 4:2" (VED, following R. C. Trench).

The *kapelos* was a retail dealer as opposed to the *emporos* or wholesaler. It could be applied to any retail merchant or peddler, but was predominantly used for the wine merchant. Paul's verb includes the element of greed, the idea of shameful or disgraceful gain, but also the practices often associated with merchandising such as selling in short measure (cf. Amos 8:5f), tampering with or adulterating the product, as a wine merchant might buy pure wine and then water it down before retailing it. The word *kapelos* is used in the Septuagint at Isaiah 1:22 for those who mix water with wine.

For more on this word, see the brief treatments of the verb in VED, "Corrupt," A. 2; GT, 324f; AG, 403; & EDNT, II, 249; and the fuller discussions in TDNT, III, 603–605 & Trench's *Synonyms*, lxii.

Reflection on the End of Chapter 2

What a fearful responsibility rests upon those who undertake to teach the word of God! Who is sufficient? Not many. Let every teacher reflect upon the awesome responsibility involved before he goes before the people undertaking to deliver a word from God.

Paul's Apostolic Credentials (3:1–3)

1. Paul anticipates two questions arising from what he has just written (1). What are the two questions?[8]

2. In response (2), Paul presents credentials, the validity of which was beyond dispute, which in fact reduces the demand for letters of commendation (1b) to an absurdity. What were his credentials or letter of recommendation?[9]

3. Paul further elucidates the thought in verse 3. Explain how the Corinthians had become an epistle "known and read of all men."[10]

---

[8] Paul is not admitting that he has been one to commend himself (cf. 10: 12, 18). The question about self-recommendation (1a) probably refers to an accusation of opponents (cf. 5:12). Paul heads them off before they can respond to 2:16b–17 by saying: "There he goes again." The second question (1b) evidently alludes to the practice of these opponents.

[9] *You are our epistle*, i. e. our letter of recommendation, Paul says. The validity of these credentials was simply beyond dispute. The demand for a letter was pure absurdity. The conversion of the Corinthians and their existence as a church of God is the very aim of apostleship, and a sufficient demonstration of the authenticity of the apostleship of the one who brought them to faith. The Corinthians themselves were the seal of Paul's apostleship (1 Cor. 9:1f). *Written in our hearts* means imprinted on our consciousness (Meyer, Hodge), so that he had not the least doubt of his own authority. But nor should anyone else, for the Corinthians were like an epistle written also on a monument: *known and read of all men.* Not that men read what was on Paul's heart. Remember, the Corinthians were the epistle and it was not just on Paul's heart that it could be read.

[10] Christ himself made them what they were. In the figure, they were an epistle written by Christ himself. As such they were an epistle of commendation for Paul and his associates. This epistle was *ministered by us.* Paul called himself and Apollos "ministers through whom you believed" (1 Cor. 3:5). But to use the metaphor

Note continued on the next page

LESSON 3

Competence as Ministers of a New Covenant (3:4–6)

1. When Paul speaks of the confidence toward God possessed by himself and his colleagues, produced in them by Christ (4), he is evidently looking back to verses 2 & 3. Make use of these two verses to define this confidence.[11]

2. How does Paul (in 5) clarify this expression of confidence, guarding against misunderstanding?[12]

3. How is the God-given sufficiency or competence (spoken of in 5) further defined in verse 6?[13]

4a. How is the new covenant characterized? (6).

---

of this passage, Paul and his colleagues were ministers or servants through whom Christ wrote this epistle. They were the scribes he used, just as Paul himself used scribes in writing his epistles (Rom. 16:22; cf. 1 Pet. 5:12).

For the Spirit in lieu of ink as the means by which the epistle was written, see First Cor. 2:4f, 10–13; Second Cor. 1:24 with 4:6; 12:12; Gal. 3:1–5; Eph. 3:5; First Thess. 1:5; Heb. 2:3b–4; and finally, Peter's description of apostolic preachers as "them that preached the gospel to you by the Holy Spirit sent forth from heaven" (1 Pet. 1:12).

Then Paul speaks of the material on which the letter was written: *not in tablets of stone, but in tablets that are hearts of flesh.* Ink is not, of course, used on tablets of stone. Paul already has in mind the comparison to be brought out in verses 6–8. The figure is strained, for the reality is more than can be illustrated by a single figure. *Hearts of flesh* as the tablets on which the epistle was written alludes to Ezekiel 11:19 & 36:26, in which a heart of flesh is one sensitive to the impressions God wants to make, in contrast to the impenetrable heart of stone. For the latter, compare Zechariah 7:12 and references to hardening the heart (Ps. 95:8; Is. 63:17; Mark 6:52; 8:17; John 12:40; Heb. 3:8, 13; 4:7).

[11] *Such confidence* as described in verses 2 & 3; confidence founded on the credentials presented, the Corinthians themselves as his letter of commendation.

[12] Paul first raised the question: Who is sufficient (or competent)? in 2:16. Then he expressed "confidence" (3:4) with regard to himself and his associates (3:1–3). But the competence of which he is confident did not derive from himself. That is not what he is claiming. It was God who empowered him.

[13] *Ministers of a new covenant*, "such as serve a new covenant" (Meyer), "the thing to which service is rendered, i. e. to which one is devoted" (GT, 138a).

4b. Clearly the distinction is between the Mosaic law and the gospel (for see 7–11). But what is the essential difference brought out in "the letter" and "the spirit" (or better: the Spirit)?[14]

5. The last part of verse 6 specifies the reason God made them "sufficient as ministers of a new covenant" having the nature described. What is the reason the apostolic company was made sufficient as ministers of such a covenant?[15]

The Glory of the Apostolic (or New Covenant) Ministry Demonstrated by Contrast With the Mosaic Covenant (3:7–11)

Follow Paul's reasoning, in which expectation is based on superior effects. If the Mosaic covenant which ministers death came with glory (cf. Ex. 34:29–35), most certainly the ministry by which the life-giving Spirit is communicated (cf. 3) will have glory (7–8). For if the ministry which pronounces judgment against sin has glory, then certainly the ministry which provides a way for people to be righteous has even more glory (9). In fact, the former has no glory at all compared with the superior glory of the latter (10). Then the final justification of the claim with regard to the greater glory of the new covenant ministry is grounded upon the fact that it remains, whereas the other passes away (11).

1. What is "the ministration of death"? (7).[16]

2. How was its glory manifested? (7; cf. Ex. 34:29–35).

3. What conclusion is reached (in 8) from the facts presented in verse 7?[17]

---

[14] This language is discussed in an appendix at the end of the lesson.

[15] Consult Romans 7:7–25 for commentary on *the letter kills*; Romans 8:1–17 on *the Spirit gives life*. The Spirit gives life by means of God's revelation of righteousness in the gospel (Rom. 1:16f), "the law of the Spirit of life in Christ Jesus" (Rom. 8:2)—a view supported in the present context by the reference to the apostles with their message as "a savor from life unto life" (2:14–16).

[16] The Mosaic ministry is described in terms of its effect. It was a ministry which leads to death.

In letters (Grk *gramma* as in 6b) *carved* (or *engraved*) *on stones*—literal translation. Cf. Ex. 24:12; 32:15f, 19; 34:1, 4, 29; Deut. 4:13; 5:22; 9:9–11; 10:1–5.

[17] *The ministry of the Spirit* must also refer to effect (as 7a & 9)—this view being confirmed by verse 3. Hence: the ministry by which the (life-giving, 6) Spirit is communicated. With regard to the Spirit as life-giving, consult John 3:3–5 & Titus 3:4–7.

LESSON 3

4. By what process of reasoning does Paul reach the conclusion that the gospel (apostolic or new covenant ministry) is of superior glory compared to the Mosaic ministry? (9).[18]

5. How is the greatly superior glory of the new covenant ministry brought out in verse 10?[19]

6. What is Paul's final justification of his claim with regard to the greater glory of the new covenant ministry? (11).

Method and Effect of the Apostolic Ministry (3:12–18)

The Apostolic Method Consistent With "Such a Hope" (12)

1a. Explain "such a hope from the preceding context (7–11).[20]

1b. Paul and his colleagues conduct their ministry in a manner consistent with "having such a hope." What is their method?[21]

Contrast With Moses (13)

2a. We are "not as Moses," says Paul. In what way?

2b. What was the purpose of the veil? (13 with 7 & Ex. 34:29ff).

---

[18] Again the reasoning is based on the effects of the respective ministries. The ministry of one has the effect of condemnation—a judgment against (Grk *katakrisis*) the sinner (Rom. 3:9–20). The ministry of the other provides a way for sinful man to be righteous before God (Rom. 1:16f; 3:21–26; 4:3-8; Phil. 3:9). The greater effect argues for greater glory.

[19] Several years ago I was walking on the beach early one morning in St. Augustine, Florida. The sky was filled with stars. A few minutes passed and I was startled to see that they were all gone. Or were they? Actually they were still in place; but they were so far outshone by the rising sun that they could not be seen.

[20] To use language from Col. 1:27, "the hope of glory": the glory that surely comes with a ministry that communicates the Spirit (8) and righteousness (9), a surpassing glory (10), an enduring, unfading glory (11). Take note of the climax to which the line of thought beginning here leads (17–18).

[21] Grk *parresia* is primarily "freedom in speaking, unreservedness in speech" (GT, 491a); "outspokenness, frankness, plainness of speech, that conceals nothing and passes over nothing" (AG, 63b); openly and freely as opposed to secretly (Mark 8:32; John 7:4, 13, 26; 18:20); without figure (John 10:24; 11:14) or parable (John 16:25). Here this openness and unreservedness stands in contrast with Moses.

Explanation: The Veil Due to Israel's Spiritual Condition (14a)

3. What was the spiritual condition among the Israelites when Moses used the veil? (14a).[22]

Elucidation of the Spiritual Condition by Reference to the Same Veil as Covering Israel's Heart to this Day (14b–15)

4a. Paul elucidates what was said (in 14a) about Israel's spiritual condition: "for until this very day at the reading of the old covenant the same veil remains unlifted"—literally, not unveiled or uncovered (14b).[23] What reason is given at the end of verse 14 that this veil has not been taken away?[24]

4b. How does Paul explain (in 15) the way "the same veil remains unlifted" even to the present?

4c. How can the veil over present day Israel's heart be called "the same veil" worn by Moses?[25]

---

[22] The first clause of verse 14 has the effect of explaining why Moses covered the manifestation of God's glory with a veil. Observe the train of thought beginning at verse 12: "We use great boldness of speech," says Paul. We do not act as Moses did, wearing a veil to cover the glory of God manifested on his face. But do not think I am finding fault with Moses. No fault is to be found in Moses for not dealing in the open, unrestrained manner we use. You must consider the character of the people to whom Moses spoke. In fact the veil worn by Moses was a fitting representation for the veil that covered Israel's heart, and even remains until this day. That veil over the heart is what kept Israel from looking upon the glory of God, even as that glory was manifested in the old covenant, which was destined to pass away in the presence of the greater glory of the gospel. Hence the elucidation that follows in 14b–15.

[23] For the widespread agreement on this translation consult ASV margin, KJV, NKJ, NASB, NIV, RSV, AG, 55b & GT, 38b on *anakalupto*.

[24] "Because (Grk *hoti*) it is taken away (or removed) in Christ." The old covenant pointed to Christ (cf. Matt. 5:17; John 5:46f; Rom. 10:4; Gal. 3:24), and Israel did not believe in Christ. Therefore, they read the old covenant as with a veil over their heart (16). Only when Christ is accepted is the veil removed and the full glory of God clearly seen as manifested in the old covenant.

[25] Paul evidently means the same veil as was so fittingly symbolized by the veil over Moses' face, preventing the people from seeing the glory of God manifested on his

Note continued on next page

LESSON 3

The Veil Taken Away in Christ (16)

5a. This verse contains a probable, almost certain allusion to Exodus 34:34. So start by answering the question: When was Moses' veil removed?

5b. When is the veil over the heart removed, enabling one to look upon the glory of God manifested in the old covenant without obscured vision?[26]

Transition Statement Explaining Two Points in Verse 16 and Preparing for the Climax in Verse 18 (17)

6a. What is the first point from verse 16, which is explained (in 17a)?[27]

---

face; "the inward veil of which the outward veil was the symbol": "The placing by Moses of a veil over his face was in itself an action symbolical of the veil of rebellion and unbelief which curtained the hearts of the people from the true apprehension of God's glory" (Hughes).

[26] The subject of the Greek verb for *turn* (in 16) is indefinite, and that is why the versions differ so much. It could be *he* (i. e., Moses, to whom the verse alludes, with reference to the law), with the meaning: Whenever the law is directed toward Christ. But the subject of the turning could be *it* —i. e., Israel's heart. But the subject could also be *he* with the meaning a man, any man; or *one*, with the sense: whenever anyone shall turn to the Lord.

Lenski argues that since Paul has not specified a definite subject, we should leave it at that, the sense then being: "whenever there is a turning to the Lord." If one instinctively looks for the implied subject of the verb in the context, however, *heart* may be the likely candidate.

"Fortunately, however, the force of the Apostle's argument is not in dispute, namely, that the veil will be removed from the Jewish heart only when there is a turning to Christ (whether it be a turning of the individual, or of the nation, or of the law metaphorically, or of the heart)" (Hughes, 113, n. 10).

[27] The first half of verse 17 is a statement about the Lord to whom there must be a turning, explaining how one confronts the Lord. No doubt Paul has the Lord Christ in mind (for see 4:5 and especially the end of 3:14). But notice the allusion to Exodus 34:34 in verse 16. Moses' turning was to Jehovah. Paul seems to identify the Lord Christ with Jehovah, which will cease to be surprising once we find Paul calling Christ "the image of God" (in 4:4).

When Paul says *the Lord is the Spirit*, which should remind us of what has been said about the Spirit in contrast with the letter (1–11), the identity is not one of

Note continued on next page

6b. As 17a explains the first part of verse 16, 17b relates to the second part. How can liberty be explained in light of that relationship between the verses?[28]

> personality, any more than John 10:30 & 14:4–11 involve an identity of person between Father and Son. In fact the latter passage illustrates this one. To know and to see Jesus was to know and to see the Father, not that Jesus and the Father were one and the same person, but that Jesus manifested the Father, speaking his words, doing his works.
>
> Jesus and the Holy Spirit are related in the same way. The presence of Jesus with the disciples was manifested through the medium of the Spirit (John 14:16–18). The glorified Christ is the sender of the Spirit, who bears witness of him (John 15:26; cf. Acts 2:33). The Spirit, as the revealer of truth, glorifies the Christ, not speaking "from himself," but taking of the things of Christ, which are immediately explained as the things of the Father, and declaring these things (John 16:12–15). See First Cor. 2:10–16 for Paul's explanation of these concepts to the very Corinthians who are now the first readers of this passage.
>
> In sum, the Christ is manifested through the Spirit. Through the manifestations of the Spirit Jesus Christ was confronted by the Corinthians.
>
> Finally, observe that the Spirit who is identified with the Lord (in the manner explained) is immediately called "the Spirit of the Lord" (17b). Compare the interchangeable use of terminology in Romans 8:9f.
>
> So 17a explains what it means to turn to the Lord (16) and how one turns to the Lord. One meets the Lord not in a direct confrontation, but through the manifestation of the Spirit (cf. 1 Cor. 2).
>
> [28] Verse 17b completes the explanation. Notice the progression: "Whenever a turning to the Lord takes place the veil is taken away." Paul first explains how one confronts the Lord and thus turns to him—namely in the manifestations of the Spirit (17a). Then he confirms what was said about the taking away of the veil. Indeed! When one turns to the Lord the veil is taken away; for "where the Spirit of the Lord is, there is liberty." GT, 204a is precisely true to context, explaining: "liberty from Jewish errors so blinding the mental vision that it does not discern the majesty of Christ." On the one hand, this liberty involves freedom from "the ministration of death" and of "condemnation"; but on the positive side, which is most emphatic in the immediate context, free and unrestrained access to the glory of God.

LESSON 3

Climax of the Presentation With Regard to the Veil: The Position of Christians in Contrast to Unbelieving Israel (18)

7a. First who are the "we" in *we all*? We Christians? or: We apostles or preachers?[29]

7b. What is the significance of "with unveiled face" in its contrast with the veil that obscures the vision of unbelieving Israel?[30]

7c. Consider whether 4:3-6 may explain why a Christian's view of the divine glory is "as in a mirror."

7d. How is "the glory of the Lord" also illuminated by 4:3–6?

7e. What happens to Christians as they continually gaze upon the glory of the Lord?[31]

---

[29] Consult context for the answer (14 end, 16). *But we all* in contrast with whom? Sometimes in Second Corinthians *we* stands in contrast to *you*; but here *we* is in contrast to *they*, i. e. the children of Israel.

[30] Compare Moses, who removed the veil when he went before Jehovah (Ex. 34:34). This allusion to Exodus 34 accounts for the use of *face* in place of (the, perhaps after 15, expected) *heart*.

[31] Compare what happened to Moses when he spent time in the presence of the Lord (Ex. 34:29f).

Some details in verse 18: *transformed* i. e., changed into another form, from the Grk verb *metamorphoo*, from which our metamorphosis derives. It is the verb used for the transfiguration of Jesus (Matt. 17:2; Mark 9:2); also in Romans 12:2. See AG, 511 & GT, 405. For *the same image* see 4:4 and perhaps Genesis 1:27.

from glory to glory "i. e. so that this transformation issues from glory (viz. from the glory of Christ beheld in the mirror and reflected on us), and has glory as its result [or aim, Grk eis, Iam] (namely, our glory)" (Meyer). Others define: from one degree of glory to another. Thus NEB: "with ever increasing glory."

even as from the Lord the Spirit Certainly the most likely construction (after 17a). Again the Lord is identified with the Spirit in the sense indicated above. See the explanation on Pentecost (Acts 2:33; cf. Titus 3:4–7). It is through the various manifestations of the Spirit that the Lord rules and does his work. The connective *kathaper* indicates correspondence: "according as, just as, even as" (GT, 312a; cf. AG, 387a); "i. e. as might be expected from such an agent. It is a work which corresponds to the nature of its author" (Hodge).

APPENDIX: THE LETTER AND THE SPIRIT
Second Cor. 3:6

The Greek "*gramma* is properly what is 'inscribed' or 'engraven' and then what is 'written' in the widest sense" (TDNT, I, 761). So also GT, 120: "that which has been written; ... any writing, a document or record"; and AG, 165a: "a document, piece of writing." Consider several points:

The Context Leading to Verse 6

The progression of thought begins with the reference to "epistles of commendation" (1). We need no such epistles, writes Paul. To demand them of us would be ludicrous. You are our commendatory epistle, "written" in two ways: "written in our hearts," so that we need have no doubt of our own authority, with such an epistle of commendation embedded within our own consciousness; but also written as a kind of epistle on a monument in a public place, "known and read of all men," for an epistle written in the heart could not be so read (2).

The thought is elucidated by means of the explanation (in 3) that the Corinthians were known as "an epistle of Christ," i. e. written by Christ— a metaphor for their conversion and existence as a church of Christ, the very fruit apostolic work was intended to bear, so that their existence was all the epistle Paul needed to authenticate his authority as an apostle of Christ (cf. 1 Cor. 9:1f).

Paul then describes this epistle written by Christ as *(1)* "ministered by us," the scribes employed by the divine author (cf. 1 Cor. 3:5); *(2)* "written not with ink, but with the Spirit of the living God," so that the epistle is actually a communication of God himself through his own Spirit; and *(3)* written "not in tablets of stone, but in tablets that are hearts of flesh," and therefore not a writing merely external to themselves, but one impressed upon their own inner being.

"Tablets of stone" shows that the contrast between "a new covenant" and the Mosaic covenant "engraven in letters on stones" (7) was already in Paul's mind. Keep in mind also the allusion to Ezekiel 11:19 & 36:26 in "hearts of flesh."

All this which has led up to verse 6 provides a basis for understanding the contrast between "letter" (= thing written) and "spirit" (really Spirit, since it refers to "the Spirit of the living God," v. 3). In fact the new covenant

LESSON 3

is a "thing written" too; the word "written" appears twice in verses 2 & 3. The difference is that between a document written on stones, never more than an external document for most Israelites, and a writing internalized in the hearts of true believers.

Scholars like Cranfield (on Romans 7:6) explain "letter" not as equal to the law as such, but as referring to what the law had become in the hands of Judaizing legalists. In no other way can the contrast between law and grace in Romans be understood. So here. "Letter" refers to the law as understood by Paul's opponents. The law was spiritual (Rom. 7:14), but it was "weak through the flesh" (Rom. 8:3, summarizing Romans 7:7–25). The fault lay in men, not in the law.

One other observation: Paul does not think of the Spirit as being communicated directly to the heart without medium. The Corinthians were an epistle of Christ written with the Spirit on hearts of flesh. But they were an epistle "ministered by us," i. e. the apostolic spokesmen. Paul and his associates (i. e. the apostolic ministry) were the medium by which this writing was done.

Old Testament Background

Turn now to the Old Testament passages to which Paul alludes, the prophecies whose fulfillment he is explaining. The fundamental passage is Jeremiah 31:31–34, where Jehovah promises to make "a new covenant" which would not be according to the covenant made with Israel at Mount Sinai, which had been broken by Israel. In regard to the old covenant being broken, recall that when Hebrews 8:7f speaks of the fault to be found in the old covenant, the fault is that of the people under that covenant. When Jehovah goes on to explain how the new covenant would be different, the first specification is: "I will put my law in their inward parts, and in their heart will I write it."

But that was God's intention from the beginning—love of Jehovah "with the heart"; the words of the covenant "upon the heart" (Deut. 6:4–9). But it was a covenant with a physical nation like our own. The nation always had a pious element—people of faith who loved Jehovah and had his law in their hearts (e. g. Psalm 119:11, 34, 47f, 97, 103, in fact the whole psalm). But the pious element was always a minority. The covenant nation also had an unbelieving, idolatrous element. When a strong king such as Hezekiah or Josiah was on the throne and the law was being enforced, the nation would appear to return to Jehovah and his law. But the return was usually superficial. Jehovah summarized Josiah's reformation thus: Judah "has not returned unto me with her whole heart, but feignedly" (Jer. 3:10).

Jeremiah 31:31–34 must be understood against that background. The new covenant would not be a covenant with a physical nation, but with spiritual individuals having penitent hearts. (See Jer. 31:29f and the elaboration in Ezek. 18.) It would be a covenant with people who had experienced a radical conversion—a new birth (John 3:1–5). They would be a new creation (2 Cor. 5:17). They would surrender to God and keep the law, not because a police force was enforcing a law written on stones, but because God had won their hearts, they loved and trusted him, and wanted to obey. It is the difference between physical Israel and the church, a new spiritual Israel composed of believing individuals who come to the Christ (1 Pet. 2:1–10).

Jeremiah's contemporary speaks of a "new heart" and "new spirit" God would give this people. The obedience of this new people would be the consequence of the communication to them of God's Spirit (Ezek. 36:25–27).

These are the prophecies whose fulfillment is recorded in Second Cor. 3, the consideration of which in their Old Testament setting leads to the same conclusion as the context of Second Cor. 3 itself. "The letter" does not refer to the law itself as a bad thing, but to what the Jews had made of the law—a document inscribed on stones or scrolls, but not a living reality in the heart and life. The gospel, on the other hand, changes the heart and moves a person to obey not out of fear of the police, but out of faith and love toward God. In that way God communicates himself to his people. He dwells within their hearts. His law is not just external, but written on their hearts. His will has become theirs.

Other New Testament References to Letter and Spirit

This interpretation of the contrast between the letter and the Spirit is reinforced by the other occurrences of the contrast in the New Testament, Romans 2:25-29 & 7:6, especially the former, where the possession of the letter (= the written document) is in contrast to being "a doer of the law" (25), keeping "the ordinances of the law" (26), fulfilling the law (27); but is consistent with being "a transgressor of the law" (25, 27). Again the letter refers to the possession of the law as a merely external written document as opposed to real obedience and inward devotion; not the law as such, but the law as experienced by most Jews.

New Testament Uses of the Greek *Gramma*

The Greek *gramma* does not always occur in this disparaging sense. Second Tim. 3:15 applies the term to "the sacred writings which are able to make (one) wise unto salvation through faith which is in Christ Jesus." John 5:47 uses it of the writings of Moses, which bear witness of the Messiah (39, 46).

"Since the Jews so clave to the letter of the law that it not only became to them a mere letter but also a hindrance to true religion, Paul calls it *gramma* in a disparaging sense, and contrasts it with *to pneuma* i. e. the divine Spirit, whether operative in the Mosaic law, Ro. 2:29, or in the gospel, by which Christians are governed, Ro. 7:6; 2 Co. 3:6 sq." (GT, 120 on *gramma*).

Law as Opposed to Grace in Paul's Writings

When law and grace are set in opposition (e. g. Rom. 6:14b) the term law is not precisely equivalent to the Mosaic legislation, which was not all law, but had an element of grace in the sacrificial system by which penitent man could remain in fellowship with God despite his sins (violations of law). The definition of law in writings such as Romans was influenced by the view of law held by Paul's opponents, whose view of law was in conflict with grace; it ruled out grace and the need of grace. For them justification had become a human achievement, wholly dependent upon man's doing, his obedience to law.

A very superficial notion of the demands of law went with this view. Jesus' exposition of the true application of the law corrected the traditional understanding (Matt. 5). Consider the shallow view of law held by the young ruler (Matt. 19:16–22); and the Pharisee who was so pleased with himself, saw no need of mercy and did not ask for forgiveness, since he did not see himself as a sinner (Luke 18:9–14). Such views isolated law from any element of grace, and when Paul deals with them he starts with law as understood by his opponents. But Mosaic legislation was not all law in this sense. It combined grace and law.

LESSON 4
Second Corinthians 4:1–5:10

TREASURE IN JARS OF CLAY
SECOND COR. 4:1–5:10

Paul continues his discussion of the apostolic ministry, which began at 2:12 and continues through 7:16. The heading of this subsection comes from 4:7. Emphasis falls first on the treasure of which he speaks (4:1–6) and then upon the fragile clay pottery in which that treasure was placed (4:7–15).

The Treasure Entrusted to Paul and His Associates (4:1–6)

The Apostolic Method (1–2)

The opening words resume the thought of 3:12 with regard to the manner in which Paul preached the gospel (cf. also 2:17).

1. Take note of the connection. The Greek for *therefore*[1] means: "for this cause; for this reason; therefore; on this account; since this is so" (GT, 134); the reason or cause being found in what precedes. For what reason or cause?[2]

2. *Having this ministry* also requires reaching back to the previous chapter for explanation. What ministry?[3]

3. These things being so, *we do not faint* or *lose heart*, says Paul. The most literal meaning of the Greek verb is "to behave badly in," and hence to fail at one's duty from weariness or despair.[4] Paul continues

---

[1] Grk *dia touto*: on account of this.

[2] "Since the Christians are so highly privileged as was specified in 3:17, 18" (Meyer).

[3] The new covenant ministry (3:6), "the ministration of the Spirit" (3:8), "the ministration of righteousness" (3:9), which has such surpassing glory (3:7–11) and brings such glory to all Christians (3:18).

[4] See GT, 166a, AG, 215, and Grundmann in TDNT, III, 486 for the Greek *egkakeo*. "The verb implies worthlessness for the work of this ministry as when men lose heart and despair and resort to questionable means and thus become *kakoi*, unfit for their task" (Lenski).

LESSON 4

by illustrating the sort of bad behavior to which one might resort as he loses heart or despairs (2a). What sort of methods had Paul renounced?[5]

4. In contrast to such dishonorable methods, what one method did Paul use to commend himself to others? (2b).[6]

Explanation with Regard to the Unbelieving (3–4)

1. How is this section connected with what has been said about the apostolic method?[7]

---

[5] *The hidden things of shame* = "what one conceals from a feeling of shame" (AG on *aischune*, 25b); "the things that are hidden out of a sense of shame" (AG on *kruptos*, 454a). Reference to dishonorable methods, as elucidated by the following clauses. Greek *panourgia* (craftiness) combines words for *all* and *work*: literally, "all-working," "readiness to do anything" (AG, 608a); ready and willing to do anything, however unscrupulous, to achieve one's purpose; of those who will "stop at nothing" (Barrett). The Greek verb in *handling the word of God deceitfully* is *doloo*, meaning "falsify, adulterate" (AG, 203); "*to corrupt* ... (in this case) divine truth by mingling with it wrong notions" (GT, 155a). (See on 2:17 for the distinction between this verb and the synonym used there.) Verse 2a pictures men willing to do anything in order to commend themselves to and thus gain the crowd. Paul had only one method (2b).

[6] "The open proclamation of the truth" (AG on *phanerosis*, 853a) is opposed to "the hidden things of shame." A clear contrast to Paul's opponents, "who accused the apostle of self-praise (3:1), but on their part not merely by letters of recommendation, but even by intrigues (*en panourgia*, 11:3, 12:16; Eph. 4:14; Luke 20:23) and by adulteration of the gospel sought to make themselves honoured and beloved among others" (Meyer). *Every man's conscience* refers to the human capacity to render a moral judgment.

Paul and his associates had one and only one way to commend themselves to others. If men hardened themselves against it, still their method remained the same. This method was used *in the sight of God*, who was understood to be the witness of all human actions, whose vision pierces through every veil.

[7] The idea of a veil over the gospel would seem to be inconsistent with Paul's protestation about the apostolic method (1–2): "We have renounced the hidden things of shame." We use an open proclamation of the truth to commend "ourselves

Note continued on next page

2. How does Paul explain the phenomenon that the gospel seemed to be veiled to some, despite the openness of the apostolic method?[8]
3. Explain Satan's method in light of Second Cor. 11:3, 13–15.[9]
4. What is said to be his purpose? (4)[10]

The Reason for Satan's Veil: The Content of Apostolic Preaching (5–6)
1. How is this explanation connected with what was said in verse 4 about Satan's purpose in blinding the minds of unbelievers?[11]

---

to every man's conscience in the sight of God." Yet many people did not recognize Paul's message as the truth, and a veil seemed to enshroud the gospel and to prevent them from seeing the glory of God manifested in it. But this situation was no evidence against Paul's claim with regard to method. The veil was not a matter that the good news was not being openly and clearly proclaimed. It was a veil over the hearts of the unbelieving, the same sort of veil that enshrouded the heart of the children of Israel at the reading of the old covenant (3:12–18). The fault was not in the gospel or in Paul's method, but in them.

[8] *Veiled* would imply: covered up, hidden from view (Grk *kalupto*, GT, 323a; AG, 401a), so that its truth is not recognized (contrast Matt. 10: 26f). Paul explains this phenomenon in verse 4. *The god of this world* is Satan, so-called because of the control he exercises over the minds of people who fulfill his will (cf. Matt. 4:8f; John 12:31; 14:30; 16:11; Eph. 2:2; 6:12; First John 5:19).

[9] He has ministers which he uses to deceive and mislead, and thus to blind the mind and to obscure the truth as with a veil.

[10] Compare 4:3–4 with 3:18 for several connections of thought.

[11] Paul introduced this devilish activity (4) as explaining the veil over the gospel in the case of those who perish (3). Satan has blinded their minds, so that they may not see the light, etc. He does not want them to see this light, to be illuminated by it. So he blinds their minds. The light is that of "the gospel of the glory of Christ, etc." That is the light Satan wants to keep from people, and so in this way he veils the gospel in the case of unbelievers. Paul continues the explanation of Satan's purpose by saying it is precisely this which we preach—not ourselves, but Christ Jesus as Lord. That explains why Satan wants to obscure Paul's gospel. It contained precisely the thing he wanted to keep from people.

LESSON 4

2. Verse 6 begins with the conjunction "for" or "because,"[12] and supplies the reason Paul's preaching is as said in verse 5. What is that reason? In other words, what lies behind the apostolic preaching?[13]

"This Treasure in Vessels of Clay" (4:7–15)

The Fact and Its Purpose (7)

1. Consult the previous verses (3–6, esp. 6) to explain *this treasure*.

2a. *Vessels of clay* is a metaphor, of course, but for what?[14]

---

[12] Paraphrase of verse 6: "because (Grk *hoti*) the Creator God, who one time commanded light to shine out of darkness (Gen. 1:3) has now shined in our hearts for the purpose (Grk *pros*) of illumination (Grk *photismos* as in 4), which consists in knowledge (genitive of apposition, Barrett) of the glory of God in the face of Jesus Christ."

[13] Pay close attention to pronouns. *We* (5) is not we Christians, but we preachers; we spokesmen for God. *Who shined in our hearts* (6) refers to revelation communicated to the apostles (cf. Gal. 1:16). Observe the contrast between "we" and "us," on the one hand, and "you" on the other in 7–15. *To give the light of the knowledge etc.* is literally "for (*pros*) illumination etc." The shining in the hearts of the preachers was for the purpose of providing illumination for others. Again, consult Galatians 1:16.

Now make some other connections. Christ is *the image of God*, according to verse 4. The glory of God is reflected in the face of Jesus Christ (6) as once that glory was seen on the face of Moses (3:7). But Paul does not mean to say we literally see the face of Christ. What is seen, as the aim and intent of the inspiration of the apostles, is *the light of the knowledge of the glory of God in the face of Jesus Christ* (6). *With unveiled face* Christians behold *as in a mirror the glory of the Lord* (3:18), that glory being mirrored in the gospel preached by Paul (4:3–5). Thus "the face of the Lord is beheld in the gospel as the reflection of the divine glory" (Meyer). Cf. John 14:7–11.

[14] "Clay jars" (NRSV); "jars of clay" (NIV). Grk *ostrakinos*, "*made of clay, earthen*: ... with the added suggestion of frailty, 2 Co. 4:7" (GT, 457b).

Grk *skeuos*, "a vessel ... *osrakina skeue* is applied to human bodies, as frail, 2 Co. 4:7" (GT, 577b); "subject to the lot of being easily destructible" (Meyer). Here "as a symbol, denoting breakableness" (AG on *astrakinos*, 587b), used for "the human

Note continued on next page

2b. Use the following verses to explain the points emphasized by the choice of this expression.

3a. What was the divine intent or purpose of placing such a magnificent treasure in common clay pots?

3b. Use context (1–6) to explain *the power*.

Illustration of the Weakness and Fragility of the Vessels in Which God's Glory is Manifested (8–10)

1. What in these verses illustrates Paul's use of the metaphor "vessels of clay"?[15]

2. What in the situation would demonstrate that "the exceeding greatness of the power" had to be of God?

---

body" (AG on *skeuos*, 754a), which is "of the earth, earthy" (1 Cor. 15:47; cf. Gen. 2:7; Job 33:6). The metaphor is frequent in Scripture (Job 10:9; Is. 29:16; 45:9; 64:8; Jer. 18:6; 19:1, 11; Lam. 4:2; Rom. 9:20f). "Clay vessels are cheap, utterly common, the least valued, used with small care, bound to break sooner or later" (Lenski).

[15] *Pressed on every side, yet not straitened.* Grk *thlibo* has the idea of pressure; to be oppressed or hard pressed. Grk *stenochoreo* is to be in a narrow, cramped space. Pressure everywhere, but not so great that all escape is cut off. God's power was at work, limiting the damage, making them sufficient for the task.

Perplexed, yet not unto despair. Grk *aporeo*: "be at a loss, in doubt, uncertain" (AG, 97); to be so without resources as "not to know which way to turn" (GT, 66b). Grk *exaporeo* is the same word, but strengthened by the preposition at the beginning (as with our "tired" and "tired out"): "to be utterly at a loss, be utterly destitute of measures or resources, to renounce all hope, be in despair" (GT, 221b); "an intensive compound meaning to be perplexed to a hopeless degree." "To be at the end of man's resources is not to be at the end of God's resources" (Hughes)— which may explain the use of the same word in 1:8.

Pursued. Acts 17:13 & 26:11 are examples of Christians being hunted down as a prey. *Yet not forsaken,* or "abandoned to the pursuing foe" (Bernard).

Smitten down, yet not destroyed. Grk *kataballo* is actually to cast or throw down; with *apollumi* used as in Matt. 2:13; 12:14; et. al. of being put to death physically. Acts 14:19 may be the best illustration in Paul's experience.

LESSON 4

3a. The climax is reached in verse 10: What do Paul and his co-workers bear about in the body at all times?[16]

3b. For what purpose?[17]

Confirmation and Elucidation of Verse 10 (11)
How is the thought of verse 10 partially explained by verse 11?

Result (12)
1. Connect this verse with the purpose (*that*) clauses of verses 10 & 11. This verse indicates the result of the danger and suffering. Point out the relation between purpose (10f) and result (12), in which the divine purpose is realized.
2. Death in these verses is physical, of course. But what about life? What is the evidence of verse 12 on the nature of the life under consideration?

Explanation: The Faith That Moves the Messengers to Speak, Despite the Suffering and Dying (13–14)
1. Clearly the connection of thought is with the great price that had to be paid by God's spokesmen in order to bring life to the Corinthians (and others like them). Note the contrast with what precedes: "But ... we

---

[16] Greek *nekrosis* is actually "a putting to death" (GT, 424a; AG, 535b) rather than just a dying. For *always* compare Paul's statement: "I die daily" (1 Cor. 15:31). He lived in constant danger of death. The *dying of Jesus* borne by the apostles is to be explained like "the sufferings of Christ" in 1:5 (cf. Col. 1:24; 1 Pet. 4:13 in context of verses 12–16). Reference to sufferings borne for the sake of Jesus (Matt. 5:11; 10:22, 39; 16:25; here at v. 11); due to identity with the name of Jesus (John 15:21; Acts 5:41).

[17] The thought of verse 10 is elucidated and confirmed in verse 11. But the idea of *the life of Jesus* is not clear until verse 12. Reference is to the life, the real spiritual life that is in Jesus, despite and in fact even due to his death (cf. John 1:4; 3:15f, 36; 5:21, 24–26; 6:35, 47–51, 63, 68; 8:12; 11:25f; 14:6).

believe, and therefore also we speak." Despite the cost, we go on speaking. How could they do it? What is Paul's explanation?[18]
2. What is meant by "the same spirit of faith" (13)?[19]
3. Verse 14 explains the content of that faith which moved them to go on speaking, despite the cost. What was their certain confidence?[20]

---

[18] These two verses explain the faith that moved these spokesmen for God to speak, despite the suffering and dying, and thus to bring the words of life to the Corinthians. It is the same faith as reflected in Psalm 116:10. Like the psalmist, says Paul, we believe and therefore speak, knowing, as we do so, that God will raise us from the dead and present us with you. Though death is at work in us so that life may be manifested "for your sakes" (15), and thus work in you (12), this spirit of faith moves us to speak, with the certain confidence that we shall be raised from the dead and thus share in the ultimate victory with you.

The connection will be clear if we take away all modifying clauses from 13f and leave only the principal sentence: But we believe and also speak. Now link 13f with 12: "So death works in us, but life in you. But ... we believe and also speak." The connection can be paraphrased thus: Even though death is at work in us as the price of bringing life to you, we believe and therefore speak. The content of that faith, *what* was believed, enabling and moving them to speak, is explained in 14.

The point in verse 12 which requires the explanation in 13f is not the life at work in the Corinthians—for who would not want to make possible such life for others?—but the death at work in the apostolic spokesmen as the means of producing such a result. What could move anyone to speak, when the cost was so great? Paul answers in 13f.

[19] For this use of "spirit" compare First Cor. 4:21 & Galatians 6:1.

[20] Recall Paul's previous reference to "God who raises the dead" (1:9) in its similar context.

shall raise up us also with Jesus, i. e. in association with (Grk *sun*) him, though not at the same time (cf. 1 Cor. 15:20–23; 2 Tim. 2:11f).

and shall present us with you. Death works in us and life in you (12). But we shall arise and be presented with you (cf. 1 Thess. 4:15–17). *Present*, as the soldiers presented Paul to the governor (Acts 23:33). On this presentation cf. 11:2; Eph. 5:27; Col. 1:22, 28; Jude 24f.

Note continued on next page

LESSON 4

Elucidation of "Us With You" in Verse 14 (15)

1a. Paul expands upon the idea that God would not just present us, but that he would "present us with you" (14, on which see footnote): *For all things are for your sakes* or *on account of you* (Grk *dia*). What details of the passage (10, 11, and especially 12) have already prepared us to understand this point?

1b. *All things* is preceded by the article in the Greek; hence not all things generally, but specifically and definitely, *all the things* of which Paul has spoken in verses 7–14. What then are these specific things that he has in mind?[21]

2. Paul then describes the purpose that was at work in all his struggles for them. What was that purpose?[22]

Consequence Following From the Certainty of the Resurrection and Future Glory (14f): Daily Renewal of the Inward Man (4:16–18)

Connection

This passage is linked to what precedes by the word *Wherefore* or *Therefore*, meaning "on which account" or "for which reason" (Grk *dio*). What is that reason, which is given in verses 14f?

This joyful association with his converts in this presentation (cf. 1 Thess. 2:19f) is the climax in the expression of confidence which moves Paul to continue to work and to speak despite the afflictions (13f) (Meyer). "The association expressed by *sun* is not only that of fellow believers raised up together but of an apostle and of ministers of Christ raised up together with those whom they brought to Christ and kept with him" (Lenski).

[21]Certainly the afflictions and sufferings described in 7–14. All these things were endured for the sake of the Corinthians (and others like them, of course)—i. e., that they may have life (12).

[22] Indicated by the *that* (Grk *hina*) clause: *that the grace, being made more by being extended to more* (cf. 1 Cor. 9:19), *may cause the thanksgiving* (i. e., for the benefits of grace) *to abound etc.* (increase, be greater or more abundant, since more people would be giving thanks). The more converts, the greater the praise. For similar concepts cf. 1:11 & 9:10–14.

Consequence Following From That Reason (16)

1. What is the negative aspect of the consequence following from the reason given (in verses 14f)?[23]

2. What is the positive aspect?[24]

Explanation with Regard to the Process of Daily Renewal (17)

The process of renewal is elucidated by showing the connection between the two opposites of 16b. The ground for the statement in 16b is "the glorious eternal result of temporal suffering" (Meyer).

What is going on all the while that accounts for the daily renewal of the inward man?[25]

Description of Those for Whom This Explanation (17) is True (18)[26]

1. Afflictions have such an effect (17) only for certain persons (18a). How are such persons characterized in 18a?

2. What reason is given (in 18b) for this fixation on the things unseen rather than the things seen?

---

[23] *We faint not*, as in verse 1, except there grounded upon the glory of the apostolic ministry, whereas here upon the conviction with regard to the resurrection, and in spite of the struggles discussed in verses 7–12.

[24] *Decaying* refers to the process of deterioration due to the sufferings and persecutions. *Renewed* means made new. Paul refers to a process of daily renewal.

[25] Greek for *works* is *katergazomai*, which means "a. *to perform, accomplish, achieve*: ... b. *to work out*, i. e. *to do that from which something results*" (GT, 339a); "*bring about, produce, create*" (AG, 421b); hence the NASB: "is producing." Affliction thus becomes a tool of the divine purpose. Cf. Rom. 5:3–5; 8:28; Jas. 1:2–4.

[26] The connection is indicated in various ways by different translations: "while" (KJV, ASV, NASB); "since" (Meyer) or "because" (RSV). The Greek is a genitive absolute, literally something like: "we being such persons as look etc."

LESSON 4

Elucidation of the Idea of Vision Fixed on Unseen, Eternal Realities: The Eternal Home (5:1–10)

Longing for the Eternal Habitation (1–4)

1a. Take note of the connection with the preceding passage (4:16–18). What reason is given for focusing on the unseen, eternal things? (1).[27]

1b. What are the two buildings that are contrasted in verse 1?[28]

1c. What is the "building from God"?[29]

2. The next verses (2–3) provide further reason for focusing on the unseen: The inward longing arising from present difficulties. What do the experiences of Paul and his colleagues produce in them?[30]

---

[27] *For we know etc.* supplies the reason we look at the eternal, unseen things. It is a knowledge based on divine revelation. The objective certainty of the eternal dwelling from God (1) will then be followed by the subjective longing (2–3).

[28] *The earthly house* is only a *tabernacle* or *tent*, a temporary dwelling, referring to the fleshly body in which man lives, the "outward man" which perishes (4: 16). Compare the idea of an earthly sojourn or pilgrimage found in First Peter 1:1, 17; 2:11–12. Peter also spoke of death as "the putting off of (his) tabernacle" (2 Pet. 1:14). Greek for dissolve or destroy is *kataluo*. Here with reference to the dismantling or taking down of a tent (AG, 414); perhaps better, the collapsing of a tent. Paul has spoken of all he and his companions have suffered in the body (4:7–18). But even if that tent completely collapses, and their earthly existence came to an end, they would not face such an event in despair as though it were the final end of all existence. For they would have *a building from God*, a permanent and substantial building as opposed to a tent, the Greek *oikodome* here being "used of the heavenly body, the abode of the soul after death" (GT, 440), but rather: "after the resurrection"; therefore better: "of the glorified body of the departed Christian" (AG, 559a). See First Cor. 15:35–58 on the resurrection body. The present tense is probably to be explained with Meyer, as referring to an ideal possession from the time of death, which is not, however, realized until the resurrection.

[29] Draw upon the entire context (1–10), even reaching back to 4:7–18 to decide the question whether reference is to a mansion in heaven or the spiritual, heavenly body that will replace the old earthly body (cf. also 1 Cor. 15:35–58).

[30] Now Paul combines (2–4) the metaphor of a garment with that of a building.

3. Verse 4 provides further explanation and more precise definition. What clarification does Paul make?[31]

Ground of the Longing (5) It is not mere wishful thinking!

1a. What is meant by *this very thing*, for which none other than God himself prepared us?[32]

1b. How does that already give foundation to the longing Paul has described?

2. What is the proof or guarantee to which Paul appeals in 5b?[33]

Effect on the Lives of Those Who Hold Such Hope (6–10)

1. *Therefore* (Grk *oun*) links these verses to the confidence Paul has just expressed. So what is the connection between these verses and what precedes?

2. What is the attitude toward death which follows from the hope set forth in the previous verses? (6–8).

2a. The whole development of thought in these verses leads to an expression of preference. What is the preference expressed by Paul in verse 8?

2b. What is meant by being *absent from the body* (contrast 6), and *at home with the Lord*? (8).

2c. What two points are mentioned in verse 6 as lying behind this expression of preference?[34]

---

[31] The object of longing was not simply escape from this life, but to have the greater life in the heavenly habitation. *What is mortal* (i. e., subject or liable to death) is from the Greek *thnetos* as in 4:11. *Swallowed up* as in 2:7. Greek *katapino* means "*drink down, swallow* ... figuratively *swallow up* with total extinction as a result": used here, First Cor. 15:54 and Psalm 106:27 (AG, 416; cf. GT, 335b). *Of life* is literally *by* (Grk *hupo*) life.

[32] See RSV, NASB & NKJ for the translation "prepared us." Greek *katergazomai* is "to fashion, i. e. render one fit for a thing" (GT, 339a); "prepare someone for something ... (here:) for this very purpose" (AG, 421b).

[33] *The earnest of the Spirit* as in 1:22. God has already made the deposit which guarantees the full payment.

[34] Grk *tharreo* is "be confident, be courageous" (AG, 352a)—the positive side of what was stated negatively in 4:1,16. Grk *endemeo* (at home) in verses 6, 8 & 9:

Note continued on next page

2d. What explanation of being *absent from the Lord* while *at home in the body* is given in verse 7?[35]

3. What is the ambition or aim in life of those who hold such a hope as set forth in this passage? (9).[36]

4. What is the motivation behind such an aim, according to verse 10?

4a. We shall not just appear in judgment, but *be made manifest before the judgment-seat*. Use Romans 2:16, First Cor. 4:5 and Hebrews 4:13 to explain.

4b. Illustrate *the judgment-seat* by reference to Matthew 27:19, John 19:13, Acts 18:12, 16f & 25:6, 10, 17.

4c. What is to be the basis of judgment?[37]

---

literally "to be among one's own people, dwell in one's own country, stay at home" (GT, 214a). Grk *ekdemeo* (absent) also in 6, 8 & 9: "*to go abroad*; hence univ. *to emigrate, depart ... to be* or *live abroad*" (GT, 193b).

[35] Greek *eidos* is "properly that which strikes the eye, which is exposed to view;" hence the thing seen rather than the act of seeing; in Second Cor. 5:7, "the visible appearance (of eternal things)" (GT, 172). Faith, on the other hand, treats as reality things hoped for, though yet future, and things real, though unseen (cf. Heb. 11:1).

[36] Greek *philotimeomai*: "have as one's ambition, consider it an honor, aspire" (AG, 861); or perhaps: "to strive earnestly, make it one's aim" (GT, 655).

Whether at home or absent relates to the body, at home in the body or absent from the body, i. e. whether we shall be among those living or dead at the return of the Lord. Whatever the case may be, verse 9 defines our aim.

[37] Each one receives *the things* done *through* or *by means of* (Grk *dia*) *the body*. Perhaps we should appeal to Exodus 21:23-25, Lev. 24:17–21 & Deut. 19:21 for illustration.

According to what he hath done is literally *with a view to what he did* (aorist tense), the whole life being treated as a unity. Accordingly, this clause is then elucidated by use of the Greek neuter singular: *whether good or bad*. Not a multiplicity of individual deeds, but the character as a whole will be evaluated. The central notion of the Greek *phaulos* (evil) is worthless, i. e. good for nothing (GT, 650; AG, 854; Trench, *Synonyms,* 317). *Good* (Grk *agathos*) would then mean beneficial. The judgment will be "an assessment of worth" (Hughes).

LESSON 5
Second Corinthians 5:11–6:10

THE MINISTRY OF RECONCILIATION
SECOND COR. 5:11–7:16

This section is directly related to the previous section, the awareness of the accountability to Christ (5:10) being the motive behind the effort of Paul and his assistants to persuade men ("therefore" in 5:11). Paul proceeds from there with explanations regarding the ministry of reconciliation entrusted to them, and especially as that ministry affected their relations with the Corinthians.

The Work of the Gospel Summarized (5:11)

1a. What connection with the preceding verse is indicated by *therefore*?

1b. What is the motivation behind the work of Paul and his companions?

1c. How is that motivation explained by the reference back to verse 10?[1]

1d. Thus motivated, how is their work summarized?[2]

2. As they did that work, what awareness did Paul have about their relation to God?[3]

---

[1] *Knowing therefore the fear of the Lord*, as the judge to whom they, and in fact *all*, were accountable (10). *Therefore* connects verse 11 with the preceding verse: *Since this is so*, i. e. what was just said. Under the influence of this fear, this sense of accountability to the Lord Christ, they acted.

[2] *We persuade men* summarizes "the great task of the gospel ministry" in trying to bring people to Christ (Lenski; cf. Acts 17:4; 18:4; 19:8, 26; 26:28; 28:23). See also Paul's description of the apostolic ministry in verses 18–20.

[3] Twice before Paul has spoken of his ministry as being conducted "in the sight of God" (2:17; 4:2; cf. also 1:23).

LESSON 5

3. What hope did he also entertain with regard to the Corinthians?[4]

The Ministry of Paul and Associates Not Self-serving (5:12–13)

1. After verse 11, what criticism does Paul anticipate? (12; cf. 3:1).

2. What was Paul's purpose in providing explanations about himself and his ministry (12)[5] ?

3. Explain Paul's characterization of his critics (in 12) by making reference to such passages as 3:1; 11:12–15, 18, 22 (cf. also John 7:24; 8:15).

4a. Paul and his companions certainly deserved to have the Corinthians stand up for them. Verse 13 provides a reason for answering their opponents. What is that reason?[6]

4b. Consider 13 in context. See if you can suggest an explanation for the alternatives Paul proposes here, in light of the previous statement (12)

---

[4] He had been worried about them, not only with regard to how they might have reacted to his first letter (cf. 2:3f, 12f) but also because of the toleration of his opponents among them, such critics as mentioned in verse 12, false teachers who wanted to discredit him and drive a wedge between himself and the Corinthians (cf. 1:17; 5:12; & throughout chs. 10–13). But the Corinthians certainly knew enough about him to appreciate his integrity (cf. 1:12–14), and after Titus' report (ch. 7) he felt confident he did not need to commend himself and his associates to them except as indicated in verse 12.

[5] *But as giving you occasion etc.* The conjunction *alla* (but) introduces a partial exception to what was said, somewhat as used in 1:13; it could be translated "except" as AG renders in 1:13 (p. 38a). Again consider AG, 38b (Section 2) where *alla* is explained as "taking back or limiting a preceding statement," with Mark 14:36, Rom. 5:15, & First Cor. 7:7; 9:12 cited. Paul is saying, "We are not again commending ourselves unto you, except as giving you occasion etc." The fact is, he was commending himself in the sense explained (cf. 4:2b & 6:4). But any apparent self-commendation was not self-serving but only intended to arm the Corinthians with the information needed to answer his opponents.

[6] The point is: Paul and his associates were entirely free from self-interest, no matter how their conduct was interpreted.

and other verses that reveal Paul's feelings when drawn into competition with his critics and "glorying" was necessary (parenthetical statements in 11:21 & 23).[7]

A Ministry Controlled by the Love of Christ (5:14–15)

1. What is Paul's explanation of the disinterested and selfless behaviour described in verse 13? (14a).[8]

---

[7] Grk *existemi* means "to be out of one's mind, beside one's self, insane" (GT, 224a; cf. AG, 276); here in contrast with being of sober mind. Some think Paul must be referring to a charge against him (as in Acts 26:24; cf. Mark 3:21). But when Paul is drawn into competition with his opponents, he feels such glorying is not only foolish, but irrational (2 Cor. 11:21, 23), necessary though it may be since the Corinthians had "compelled" him (12:11). The context is the same here. So it may be that he already has in mind such "foolish" boasting as he was compelled to do, and perhaps anticipating how someone may feel about his own "glorying" (chs. 10–13, but nearer to hand, the present section 5:11–6:10, esp. the characterization of his ministry in 6:1–10). They may think he is being irrational, out of his senses. He feels the same way himself. But such foolishness and irrationality was necessary in the circumstances. It was not done for selfish purpose, but in the service of God. The fact is, it was not really foolish or irrational, since a rational purpose was behind it.

To be *of sober mind* is the opposite of being out of one's senses. Grk *sophroneo* means *to be of sound mind; to be in one's right mind; be reasonable, sensible, serious, keep one's head* (AG, 802a; GT, 612b similarly). Whatever might appear to be the case, the rational purpose behind the "glorying" shows that this is the real truth of the matter. What seemed to be irrational was really the product of calm and sober judgment. Most of the Corinthians would doubtless see Paul's attempt in this way—not as the ravings of one out of his senses, but as coming from one of sober mind and being for their benefit.

It is unto you means in your interest; for your benefit; not self-serving (cf. 12:19). So however Paul's behavior in this matter be interpreted, they had good reason to stand up for him against his opponents (12).

[8] *For the love of Christ constrains us* (KJV, ASV) or *controls us* (RSV, NASB, REB). Greek *sunecho* is literally "to hold together," as with constraints. It is used in

Note continued on next page

LESSON 5

2. Does "the love of Christ" (14a) mean his love for us or our love for him? Support your answer from the context.[9]

3. What judgment or decision reached by Paul and his companions was behind the controlling power of this love? (14b).[10]

4. The content of the judgment reached by Paul and his associates begins with the statement *that one died for all* (14b), but then runs to the end of verse 15. Understanding that, two other questions will bring us to the end of the thought. First: What must be the meaning of the death of Christ if the death of all follows from the fact that *one died for all*? Or to put it another way: if the death of all was included in the death of the one?[11]

5. Verse 15 then completes the explanation of the judgment or decision about the meaning of the death of Christ, which lies back of the being controlled by the love of Christ. The statement *he died for all* is re-

---

Philippians 1:23 where Paul said he was "in a strait between the two"—as GT, 604 explains: "I am hard pressed on both sides, my mind is impelled or disturbed from each side." The word is used of the pressure of a crowd on one (Luke 8:45); the pressure of a city under siege by enemies (Luke 19: 43); of a prisoner held in custody (Luke 22:63). The thought here is not so much that the love of Christ urges, impels or motivates, as that it controls or confines; which is the reason for the selfless behavior described in verse 13.

[9] Consult also Galatians 2:20.

[10] *Because we thus judge* is literally: *having judged this*, or *having come to this decision* or *judgment* (aorist participial clause *krinantas touto*), the judgment explained by what follows. The verb *krino* is used to mean: "reach a decision, decide, propose, intend" (AG, 451). The same verb is used of Paul's determination in 2:1. So the relationship between the clauses is this: "Having arrived at this judgment," we were ever after under the control of Christ's love.

[11] The Greek preposition *huper* is primarily *on behalf of* or *for the benefit of*. But the conclusion that is drawn from the death of one *therefore all died* necessarily implies that the death was *on behalf of all* as being *in the place of all*, i. e., *as a substitute for all*. "On this ground alone is there justification for speaking as Paul does here of a logical identification of all with Christ in His death; and on this ground alone is there an adequate explanation of the constraining power of Christ's love" (Hughes). What the substitutionary death of Christ means, then, is that God sees in his death the death of all; as though we had died and thus satisfied the demand of the law for the death of the sinner.

peated in order to add a purpose clause. This purpose for which he died for all finishes the explanation of the judgment about the death of Christ. What is that purpose?[12]

6. Do you now understand why one who makes this judgment about the death of Christ would ever after be controlled by the love of Christ?

Consequence Following From This Judgment About the Death of Christ: A New View of Men (5:16–17)

Pay attention to the connecting word *wherefore*, from a Greek conjunction meaning "for this reason," "therefore" or "so then,"[13] which introduces a consequence that follows from verses 14–15. It is a consequence of the judgment arrived at with regard to the meaning of the death of Christ. Notice the return to "we."[14] The divine purpose in the death of Christ has actually been realized in the case of Paul and his assistants (Lenski). So the inference drawn here has regard to the change which this judgment about the death of Christ has produced in their thinking—the way they see things, but especially men.[15]

---

[12] *They that live* refers not to the *all* for whom Christ died, but to those who have had the effect of his death actually applied to them through baptism (Rom. 6:1–11); that is, those who have actually experienced the power of the death of Christ, and thus have fellowship in both his death and also his new resurrection life. Cf. 4:11 for the description here.

The divine purpose set forth in verse 15 explains the selfless life described in 13, for which Paul accounts by saying he and his companions were controlled by the love of Christ (14a).

[13] Grk *hoste* is "a consecutive conjunction, i. e. expressing consequence or result" (GT, 683a); having the function in both verses 16 & 17 of "introducing independent clauses" with the meaning "for this reason, therefore" (AG, 899b). Or it could be rendered "so then" (GT).

[14] The first *we* (in 16) is emphatic, being expressed rather than implied in the verb. Therefore: *we*, whatever may be true of others; or: we, as opposed to our opponents, who do know men "after the flesh" and "glory in appearance" (11).

[15] The Greek for *henceforth* (16) is literally *from the now*, hence "from now on" (NKJV; NASB; GT, 430b; AG, 546a). But verse 16 is an inference from the judgment

Note continued on next page

1. What change of view followed from the decision Paul and his assistants reached about the death of Christ? (16a).[16]
2. In particular, how did their view of Christ change? (16b).
3. What further consequence ("wherefore") follows from the change in the way Christ is known? (17).[17]
4. How does Paul elaborate or explain the idea of a new creature? (17bc).[18]

The New Creation Accomplished by Reconciliation (5:18-19)

Verse 17 ended by calling attention to a remarkable fact: "Behold, new things have come into existence." Verses 18f explain how the Creator brought this new creation into existence. In the course of the explanation Paul returns to the apostolic ministry "which connected him with the Corinthians" (Lenski).

1. *All things* refers to the new things that have "come into existence" as a new creation (17). This new creation in its entirety derives from God, the Creator. But Paul does not then describe God as Creator. Instead of saying *who created us*, how does Paul characterize God? In other words, what did God do to bring this new creation into existence?

---

reached with regard to the death of Christ (14f). Therefore, the standpoint is the time they arrived at that judgment. From that moment on "our whole way of looking at people has undergone a change" (Lenski).

[16] *After the flesh* means according to human standards or "from a human point of view or as far as externals are concerned" (AG, 744a); such things as nationality, wealth, learning and social status (Meyer). Cf. John 8:15; First Cor. 1:26; Second Cor. 11:18; Eph. 6:5; Phil. 3:3f; Col. 3:22.

[17] Since they no longer see Christ from a human point of view, they also no longer see a man in Christ from that point of view, but rather as something different, a new creature. Being in Christ makes all the difference.

[18] *The old things*, i. e. the things characteristic of the old, pre-Christian life. *They are become new* is from Greek perhaps better translated: *new things have come into existence* (Grk *ginomai*). The verse speaks of a new creation rather than a transformation of the old. "The old things are passed away."

2. Consult First Cor. 7:11 to illustrate the meaning of the word *reconcile*, and then make application to the relation between man and God.[19]
3. What role was assigned Paul and his colleagues in reconciliation? (18).[20]
4. *The ministry of reconciliation* is further expounded in verse 19.[21] Explain what the ministry of reconciliation is all about by directing attention to Paul's three points:

   a. What is the positive side of the work God was doing in Christ?

   b. What is the negative side of God's work in Christ?[22]

---

[19] Grk *katallasso* involves a change in the relationship. First Cor. 7:11 is a good illustration. First the alienation, then the restored harmony—"let her return into harmony with her husband" (GT, 333b). Because of sin man was under the wrath of God (Rom. 1:18-3:20), alienated from him. But Christ was sent as the means of propitiation by which man's sin was dealt with, the wrath removed, and a new relationship of harmony and peace established. See the occurrence of this verb in Romans 5:10f, and the whole context. The other New Testament occurrences are found in Second Cor. 5:19f.

[20] *The ministry of reconciliation* is "the ministry whose work it is to induce men to embrace the offered reconciliation with God" (GT on *diakonia*, 137b).

[21] The Greek connection between verse 18 and verse 19 is an unusual combination (but found also in 11:21 and in Second Thess. 2:2). The most literal rendering of *hos hoti* would be *how that*. Various versions translate as follows: to wit (KJV; ASV); that is (RSV; NKJV); and namely (NASB); all amounting to about the same thing.

[22] Not charging sin to mankind. God was reconciling; he was not reckoning. One the positive side of God's work in Christ; the other the negative. The negative aspect is necessarily implied in reconciling, for God could not bring the world into a friendly relation to himself if he was at the same time holding their sins against them. Grk *logizomai* is to charge to one's account (GT, 37a; AG, 475b). The sins were not put to the account of mankind, but to the account of Christ (21) and he paid the price for them.

LESSON 5

c. The third element of *the ministry of reconciliation* is the deposit of "the word of reconciliation" with the messengers.[23] What would be their role in the reconciliation of the world to God?

The Word of Reconciliation (5:20–6:10)

The word *therefore* (Grk *oun*, v. 20) links 20ff to the last clause of verse 19 in the following manner: Since God has deposited in us, his apostolic spokesmen, the message of reconciliation, we are ambassadors sent forth as representatives of the government of heaven to proclaim this message to the world and thus, as was said in verse 11, to persuade men. This section summarizes the message of reconciliation and explains how Paul and his coworkers conducted themselves in a manner faithful to the trust placed in them.

Plea of the Ambassadors (5:20)

1. What is the significance of the word ambassadors?[24]
2. What was the message of these ambassadors on behalf of Christ?[25]

---

[23] The last clause of verse 19 says *God put, placed* or *deposited* (Grk *themenos*, second aorist middle nominative plural masculine participle of the verb *tithemi*) *in us* (i. e., our minds) *the word of the reconciliation*, in order that, as we soon see (20ff), the message of reconciliation might be made known to others (GT, 623a). This was God's way of getting the benefits of the reconciling death of Jesus to the world, applying it to the world. It is not enough to discover a vaccine against deadly disease. The vaccine has to be made available to those who need it, and they have to take it.

[24] Paul uses the Greek verb *presbeuo*, meaning "to be an ambassador" or "to act as an ambassador" (GT, 535b). An ambassador represents a government, and speaks with the authority of that government. The apostolic ambassadors represented Christ and spoke in behalf of Christ. Their message bore all the authority of Christ himself. It was *as though God were entreating through us,* says Paul. See TDNT, VI, 681–683.

[25] Observe that "you" in "we beseech you" is italicized as an added word not in the original. Verse 20b summarizes the message proclaimed by the apostles all over the world, and not just to the Corinthians.

Ground of the Plea: The Possibility of Reconciliation Because of God's Grace in Christ (5:21)

1. Explain 21a in light of such verses as Galatians 3:13, First Peter 2:24, and perhaps Romans 8:3.[26]
2. What was the divine purpose for which Jesus was "made sin"? (21b).[27]

The Apostolic Entreaty (6:1–2)

1. After the explanation of the divine grace which made reconciliation possible (5:21), now this apostolic entreaty in cooperation with the work of God. In what way does 6:1 relate to 5:21?
2. What can be the meaning of such an entreaty addressed to people who had already accepted God's grace and been reconciled to God?[28]
3. The plea is supported by reference to the urgency of the situation (6:2, citing Isaiah 49:8). How is the urgency of the situation brought out?[29]

---

[26] By "sending his own Son in the likeness of sinful flesh and for sin," God "*condemned sin in the flesh*" (Rom. 8:3). The cross was an execution of judgment against sin in the flesh. This judgment fell upon God's Son who "bare our sins in his body upon the tree" (1 Pet. 2:24). He thus became "a curse for us" (Gal. 3:13).

[27] Verse 21b is explained by Romans 3:21–26, 4:6–8, and Second Cor. 5:19 in this context. Sinners are justified, i. e. acquitted from sin and declared not guilty, through faith. Sins are not charged to them, and they are declared to be righteous. This judgment upon them is the righteousness of God communicated to sinners as a gift (Phil. 3:9). Bearing our sins Jesus became the concrete embodiment of sin, and we become the concrete embodiment of God's righteousness.

[28] It is a plea that the grace made known in Christ (5:21) not go for nothing, but rather have its effect in their lives; i. e. "to be doers of the word and not hearers only" (Jas. 1:22). Grk "*eis kenon* in vain, to no purpose" (AG, 427b & GT, 343b both the same). It will be helpful to consult other occurrences of the same phrase: Gal. 2:2; Phil. 2:16; First Thess. 3:5. Concerning himself Paul had written: "His grace which was bestowed upon me was not found vain" (1 Cor. 15:10, which see for context).

[29] *Now is the day of salvation* (2), with implication (1): Do not let it pass.

Characterization of the Entreaty (6:3–10) ... the manner in which the plea is made, these verses being linked to verse 1 rather than directly to verse 2. Basically the whole passage describes the way in which the ministry of reconciliation was executed by Paul and his coworkers. Try not to miss a point. We must make Paul our model for gospel ministry today.

1. *Negatively: Providing no occasion of stumbling in anything (3; cf. 1 Cor. 8:13; 9:12).* What does the purpose clause (in 3b) indicate about the importance of such conduct?

2. *Positively: In everything commending ourselves as ministers of God (4–10; contrast 3:1; 4:2; 5:12)* ... this climax apparently being already in Paul's mind in the statement of purpose in 5:12. Discuss the way in which Paul and his colleagues commended themselves as ministers of God, and the importance of so doing. What a wonderfully instructive passage for those who serve as ministers of God in their way today!

    (1) Perseverance in trying external circumstances (4–5).

    (2) Moral characteristics (6).[30]

    (3) Equipment of a preacher (7).

    (4) Contradictory responses to the ministry (8–9a). Give thought to what is meant by these contrasts.

    (5) Its paradoxical character (9b–10). See if you can explain these apparent contradictions.

---

[30] Consider whether *the Holy Spirit* is not rather *a holy spirit* (cf. 1 Cor. 7:34; 2 Cor. 7:1; 12:18) in such a list of ethical qualities.

LESSON 6
Second Corinthians 6:11–7:4

THE MINISTRY OF RECONCILIATION (5:11–7:16)
continued

The Apostle's Plea to His Beloved Children (6:11–7:4)

Paul's discussion of *The Ministry of Reconciliation (5:11–7:16)* continues. To understand this section (6:11–7:4), go back to the beginning of the larger unit and recall Paul's explanation of his purpose. His self-commendation (5:12 with 6:4), which extends through 6:10, was intended to provide the Corinthians with material they could use to stand up for him and thus to answer his opponents and critics (5:12). When these false teachers came to Corinth trying to discredit the apostle and to take the church from him, Paul should not have had to defend himself, but was compelled to do so. The church certainly knew enough about him to stick up for him, but apparently had not done so (cf. 12:11).

The material included under the above heading consists of three subdivisions (6:11–13, 6:14–7:1 & 7:2–4). The first and third are a plea to the Corinthians to open up their hearts and make room for their old teachers. But what is the meaning of this plea, and how is it consistent with the confidence and joy in the Corinthians which Paul felt after receiving the report from Titus? (7:4, 7). The apparent inconsistency is explained by the middle section (6:14–7:1).

Though the Corinthians had not been alienated from Paul and his companions (7:7, 11–12), his opponents remained in Corinth and the church seemed to be tolerating them in their midst rather than strongly rejecting and dismissing them as men who preach another Jesus and a different gospel (11:4) and are really ministers of Satan in disguise (11:13–15). The church seemed to be under the illusion that they could be faithful to the old teachers while tolerating such men in their midst. But if the church was going to fully embrace Paul and other faithful teachers, they would have to separate themselves from unbelievers.[1]

---

[1] Thus the passage (6:14–7:1) treated by liberal scholars as a foreign element at odds with the context becomes the key to understanding the whole.

LESSON 6

Plea for Enlargement of Heart to Receive the Old Teachers (6:11–13)

1. Do not miss the abruptness of this passage, coming as it does right on the heels of Paul's characterization of the way his ministry was conducted (6:3–10). The Corinthian church would certainly not dispute the description, and it leads right into the declaration of verse 11. What was the attitude of Paul and his coworkers toward the Corinthians according to this verse?[2]

2. What was the problem, then, if not the attitude of their old teachers? (12).[3]

3. In what way did Paul call upon the Corinthians to reciprocate the attitude of these old teachers? (13).[4]

Call for Separation from Unbelievers (6:14–7:1)

1. This passage will not be understood without close attention to context, in which it is sandwiched between the plea to enlarge their hearts to make room for their old teachers (in 6:11–13) and the resumption of that same plea (in 7:2). Given this context, with this negative (6:14–7:1) sandwiched between two identical positives (6:11–13 & 7:2), what is likely to be the special reference of "unbelievers" in 6:14a?[5]

2a. Explain the imagery of the unequal yoke (14a) in light of the allusion to the Old Testament (Deut. 22:10 in context of 9–11; cf. Lev. 19:19).

---

[2] They had certainly demonstrated this attitude in the way their ministry had been conducted (3–10).

[3] Grk *stenochoreo*, "*crowd, cramp, confine, restrict*, figuratively, passive *be confined, restricted*" (AG, 766b; cf. GT, 587a). The problem of restricted space was not in the hearts of the ministers, but in those they served.

[4] This passage clarifies the application of the apostolic entreaty not to receive the grace of God in vain (1). Continuing with their old teachers was the means of fruitful acceptance of grace.

[5] Paul's work in Corinth was being undermined by teachers of another type (10:1, 10–12; 11:1–4, 12–15). His eye was specially on these false teachers, but the language is broad enough to include any whose work compromises the truth of the gospel.

2b. What would be the meaning of this warning?[6]

3. Summarize the reason for the prohibition in 14a brought out in the questions of 14b–16a.[7]

4. How is the last question illustrated by the idolatry of Ahaz (2 Kings 16:10–16) and Manasseh (2 Kings 21:1–9)?

5a. The last question (16a) is supported with an explanation (16bc). Why is this question specially to the point? (16b; cf. 1 Cor. 3:16).

5b. With what promise is the concept of the church as a temple of God in agreement? (16cd; cf. Ex. 29:45f; Lev. 26:11f; Ezek. 37: 27).

5c. What is demanded as the ground of this relationship with God? (17–18; cf. Isaiah 52:11 for verse 17 and Isaiah 43:6 & Hosea 1:10 for verse 18).

6a. What exhortation follows from the promises cited in 6:16–18? (7:1).

6b. What is there about these promises that leads to the exhortation in 7:1?

Renewal of Plea for Enlargement of Hearts (7:2–4)

1. Observe how verse 2a resumes the plea in 6:11–13. That being the connection, what light is cast on the meaning and application of 6:14–7:1?[8]

---

[6] It is a warning against spiritual alliances with unbelievers.

[7] *Belial* or *Beliar* is a name for Satan or some Satanic power (cf. 11:13–15).

[8] The Grk verb *choreo* is literally "*to leave a space* (which may be occupied or filled by another), *to make room, give place, yield,*" and hence "*to have space* or *room for receiving* or *holding something.*" Here the idea is "*to receive one into one's heart, make room for one in one's heart*" (GT, 674; cf. AG, 889f). Plainly, 7:2a is a resumption of the thought of 6:11–13, which is to say that Paul had not finished the thought. The intervening passage 6:14–7:1 is no digression from the thought of 6:11–13, but deals with contrary attitudes which would prevent their doing as Paul asks in 6:11–13 & 7:2. Thus: enlarge your hearts to receive us (6:13). Do not become allied with unbelievers instead, which would prevent your doing so (6:14–7:1), but do indeed make room for us (7:2).

2. How is the resumption of this plea supported by the protestation of 7:2b?[9]

3. What clarification of this protestation is offered in 7:3a?[10]

4. In fact, what attitude did Paul and his companions have toward the Corthians, as he had already made clear? (3b; cf. 1:6; 3:2; 4:7–15; 6:11).[11]

5. Verse 4 expounds upon this positive attitude toward the Corinthians in an emotional outburst which resumes the personal narrative from 2:12–13. The reason for all the emotion expressed in this verse will be explained in the following passage (7:5–16). Compare especially 7:14 and then 9:1–5.

---

[9] The Corinthians had no reason to shut their hearts against Paul and his associates (2b; cf. 12:14–18).

[10] Paul's claim with regard to behavior toward the Corinthians was not a "back doors" way of condemning the Corinthians for their attitude toward him and his associates (3a).

[11] Verse 3b describes a fellowship that remains unbroken (contrast 6:14–7:1).

LESSON 7
Second Corinthians 7:5–16

THE MINISTRY OF RECONCILIATION (5:11–7:16)
continued

Comfort and Joy Upon Meeting Titus in Macedonia (7:5–16)

This passage explains the expressions of emotion (4), but also resumes the narrative (from 2:12f) in connection with which Paul's discussion of apostolic ministry is woven.

Explanation of Overflowing Joy on Occasion [Grk *epi* (upon) in v. 4] of Affliction (5–7)

1a. How is the emotion (in v. 4) explained in these verses?

1b. Link these verses also with the narrative broken off at 2:12f.

2. Contrast Paul's expression of distress (in 5) with the way he expresses the same feelings in 2:13.[1]

3. What caused the distress which continued even after the arrival in Macedonia? (5).[2]

4. How does this passage (esp. 6–7) also relate to the emotional outburst of praise with which this epistle begins (cf. 1:3f)?[3]

---

[1] The comparison shows that flesh does not refer to the body, for Paul's affliction was primarily mental. It refers to the whole of the human nature, existing as it now does in the form of a fleshly body.

[2] The afflictions took two forms: External struggles with opponents, whether within or without the church, and internal fears, primarily including anxieties about the Corinthians, as earlier passages have indicated.

[3] It actually explains why the epistle begins as it does. Then 7:5–16 as a whole wraps up the first major section of the epistle (chs. 1–7) into a neat package.

LESSON 7

5a. What were the two means by which God comforted or encouraged Paul and Timothy (for see 1:1) at Macedonia? (6–7).

5b. How would the coming of Titus itself be a relief and an encouragement to Paul and Timothy? (cf. 2:12f).

5c. What increased their encouragement and joy even more?[4]

Further Explanation of Paul's Joy: Repentance of the Corinthians (8–11)

Paul must be quite clear in writing to a church where false teachers were ready to pounce on any word they could turn against him. He did not take joy in their mourning and sadness as such. A surgeon can take no joy in having to inflict pain as the price of healing. But the result takes away any regret he feels over inflicting the necessary pain. So here. The infliction of pain was necessary. But Paul could take no joy in the pain. (See 1:23–2:4 for his feelings about the first epistle.) His joy arose from the repentance produced by godly sorrow.

1. What did Paul regret for a time, but no longer? (8).

2. How does Paul explain the joy he afterward felt? (9).

3. What was the effect of Paul's previous epistle? (8–9a).[5]

---

[4] All three of the nouns characterizing the Corinthians are connected with *for me*. *Your longing*, i. e. for me. What a relief to Paul! who must have wondered about the extent to which his converts were estranged from him. *Your mourning*, i. e. over the wrongs that had called forth the apostle's reproof. *Your zeal*, from the Grk *zelos*: "excitement of mind, ardor, fervor of spirit" (GT, 271a); "your ardor on my behalf" (AG, 337b). "What was so specially gratifying to him was that in a church in which he had met with so much opposition, and in which the false teachers had exerted so great and so evil an influence, the mass of the people proved themselves devoted to him" (Hodge), which is tantamount to saying: to the truth of the gospel. "Paul, the apostle, was the one for whom the Corinthians were now so zealous to defend him against any derogations, to obey him as their true leader and guide" (Lenski).

[5] Grk *metanoia* (repentance): "*a change of mind*: as it appears in one who repents of a purpose he has formed or of something he has done, ... esp. the change of mind of those who have begun to abhor their errors and misdeeds, and have determined to enter upon a better course of life, so that it embraces both a recognition of sin and sorrow for it and hearty amendment, the tokens and effects of which are good deeds" (GT, 405f; cf. AG, 512b).

4. How does Paul characterize the sorrow produced in the Corinthians by his other epistle? (9b).[6]

5. For what purpose were they "made sorry unto repentance"? (9b).[7]

6. "For" links verse 10 with what precedes. Verse 10 provides further explanation of the loss prevented by sorrow which is *according to God*. In what way does 10 provide an explanation of this matter? In other words, what was the fruit produced by *sorrow according to God* which prevented loss from being suffered by the Corinthians and therefore was not to be regretted?[8]

---

[6] Literally: *For you were made sorry according to God*. The Greek phrase *kata theon* means "in a way that accords with God ... in harmony with God" (Lenski); "agreeably to the will of God, as pleases him" (GT, 328b), "in a manner acceptable to God" (GT on *lupeo*, 383); "with the accusative of the person according to whose will, pleasure, or manner something occurs" (AG, 407a); "(you were made sorry) as God would have it" (AG on *lupeo*, 481b); "i. e. in a manner agreeable to the mind and will of God; so that God approved of their sorrow" (Hodge). So also verses 10f; the same phrase as in Romans 8:27. It was a sorrow in accord with God; a sorrow that works to fulfill divine purpose.

[7] Interesting! One usually grieves over a loss (Lenski), but not so in this case. The loss would have been suffered had Paul remained silent and not inflicted the pain and sorrow caused by the first epistle, or if his rebuke had repelled them.

[8] *Godly sorrow* is "sorrow acceptable to God" (GT on *lupe*, 383b), "sorrow that God approves" (AG on *lupe*, 482a), or perhaps better still, and literally: sorrow in accord with God; that works to fulfill divine purpose. *Works* (Grk *ergazomai*) means produces (GT, 247b); brings about or gives rise to (AG, 307a). The adjective (Grk *ametameletos*), meaning "not to be regretted, without regret" (AG, 45b; cf. GT, 32a), is nearest salvation in the text; but many connect it with repentance, which is also grammatically possible, since the idea of regretting salvation is inconceivable. But perhaps Hughes is best, treating "repentance-unto-salvation" as a grammatical unit, and "not to be regretted" as qualifying the whole phrase. Paul had formerly felt regret at the sorrow he had had to inflict by means of his first epistle (8), but no longer, after seeing the result of that sorrow (8f). The fruit of godly sorrow is not to be regretted (10a).

LESSON 7

7. But men of the world experience another kind of sorrow (10b), which does not produce repentance unto salvation. What does it produce instead?[9]

8. What has been said (in 10) about the fruit of sorrow according to God is then supported by calling attention to the concrete manifestations of such sorrow at Corinth. How had sorrow according to God manifested itself among the Christians at Corinth? (11).[10]

---

[9] The sorrow of the world is such sorrow as men of the world experience; grief over losses (GT on *lupe*, 383b) or over the consequences of sin; but not *according to God*. It is not sorrow over sin itself such as leads them to forsake sin and so does not lead to salvation. It "brings about" or "results in" death instead (GT, 339a). It "works it out"; it inevitably leads to death. Here the Greek verb is not *ergazomai* (as in 10a), but *katergazomai*.

[10] *Behold!* (Grk *idou* as in 5:17 & 6:2), Paul writes. "Look what godly sorrow has accomplished!" The verb is again *katergazomai*. Paul first said godly sorrow produces repentance unto salvation (10a); then piles up a list of the blessed fruit produced by godly sorrow (11). The list seems either to define repentance, or, more probably, to enumerate various things associated with repentance:

(1) *Earnest care*. The first meaning of Grk *spoude* is "haste" or "speed"—hence not standing around waiting, but getting down to business. Then it refers to "*eagerness, earnestness, diligence*, also *zeal* in matters of religion" (AG, 763); "earnestness in accomplishing, promoting, or striving after anything" (GT, 585). Here "namely, to efface and make amends for the offence, as opposed to their previous negligence in regard to the incestuous person" (Meyer; cf. 1 Cor. 5).

(2) *Clearing of yourselves*. Grk *apologia*: "verbal defence, speech in defence" (GT, 65b)—not a defense of their sin, but answering for or giving account of themselves by setting things right; "clearing" themselves of the charge against them by putting things right, seeking forgiveness.

(3) *Indignation* (Grk *aganaktesis*), i. e. at the disgrace of such a sin in the church; the scandal tolerated by the church; the affront to the name of God.

(4) *Fear* may combine two elements: Fear of the wrath of God, but perhaps also of the apostle's coming "with a rod" as an agent of divine judgment (1 Cor. 4:21). Cf. Second Kings 22:11; contra. Jer. 36:20–26.

(5) *Longing*. Probably as in 7, longing for the apostle, "longing after the apostle's coming" (Meyer); perhaps "to have Paul himself present in Corinth to direct everything" (Lenski).

Note continued on next page

2 CORINTHIANS 7:5–16

Comfort and Good Courage After the Report of Such Faithful Action on the Part of the Corinthians (12–16)

1. As Paul concludes, he provides further explanation with regard to the purpose of his first letter (12; cf. 8). What does he say about this matter?[11]

2a. For this reason (Grk *dia touto*), Paul continues, *we have been comforted* (13a). What is the reason (found in 12) for the comfort or encouragement?

2b. What, in addition (13b), increased the joy of Paul and Timothy (1:1)?

3. How is this joy further explained in verse 14?

4. What made Titus feel increased affection toward the Corinthians? (15).

5. What attitude is expressed toward the Corinthians as Paul closes out the matter? (16).[12]

---

(6) *Zeal*. Grk *zelos* as in 7: "excitement of mind, ardor, fervor of spirit" (GT, 271); from the verb *zeo*: "to boil with heat, be hot" (*Ibid*). Here probably more a zeal to get things set right, than merely a zeal for Paul (as in 7).

(7) *Avenging*. Grk *ekdikesis*: "vengeance, punishment" (AG, 238b; cf. GT, 194a); respecting the action taken against the sinner.

Finally, a summary in 11b: Showing themselves free from fault in every way. Grk *sunistemi* is the word used throughout the epistle (3:1; 4:2; 5:12; 6:4) for *commend*. Here defined "to show, prove, establish, exhibit" (GT, 605b); "demonstrate, show, bring out" (AG, 790b). *To be pure* is from the Grk *hagnos*, here defined as "innocent" (AG, 12a); free from guilt or fault (GT, 8a); spoken from the standpoint in time when the results enumerated have been worked out in them.

[11] *Not for his cause that did the wrong* alludes to First Cor. 5, but must be understood in a relative sense. One cannot read First Cor. 5 and understand it otherwise. The point is, a larger issue was involved than the specific problem—namely, the church's attitude toward an apostle (cf. 2:9). [The Greek indicates *your earnest care on behalf of us*; not *our care for you* (KJV).] *Earnest care* (Grk *spoude*, as in 11), as opposed to indifference toward the apostle and his associates. *Might be made manifest to you*, i. e. making them realize how important the apostle and his company were to them. But it was not just a personal matter. The crisis forced this church to decide what it wanted to be. The attitude they took toward apostolic authority would determine whether they could be a church of Christ.

[12] This attitude is important to the next section. For if Paul felt otherwise toward the Corinthians, could he even have continued with the collection?

PART TWO

The Collection for the Saints

SECOND CORINTHIANS 8 & 9

LESSON 8
Second Corinthians 8

Introduction to Chapters 8 and 9

Paul's meeting with certain apostles in Jerusalem, reported in Galatians 2:1–10, had concluded with an understanding about division of labor, but also with a request from these Jerusalem leaders "that we should remember the poor; which very thing," writes Paul, "I was also zealous to do." In fact he and Barnabas had already brought relief from the disciples at Antioch of Syria to "the brethren living in Judea" (Acts 11:27–30; 12:25).

But the project dealt with in this section of Second Corinthians went far beyond the scope of anything that had been done before. It was a great collection in which virtually all "the churches of the Gentiles" participated. We know from the references to it in Paul's epistles (Rom. 15:25–27; 1 Cor. 16:1–4; 2 Cor. 8–9) that the churches in the provinces of Galatia, Macedonia and Achaia were involved, and the listing of Paul's travel companions in Acts 20:4 (cf. 21: 29) seems to give evidence of the participation of Asia as well. The only direct mention of the collection in Acts is found at 24:17.

Romans 15:25–27 points out an important feature of this collection. It was a collection being made among Gentile Christians for the benefit of Jewish Christians in Judea. It is even treated as a matter of discharging a debt owed by Gentile Christians to Jewish Christians, the former having received the gospel from the latter. But it is at the close of the discussion in Second Corinthians that Paul is most clear about the twofold purpose he had in mind for the collection. It would, of course, "fill up the measure of the wants of the saints," but more than that, Paul hoped that a generous gift from the Gentile Christians to the Jewish Christians in Jerusalem would strengthen the bonds of unity between these two groups, cementing them into one cohesive body. We consider Paul's explanation of this purpose at Second Cor. 9:12–14.[1]

---

[1] A little later, Paul expresses doubt that the collection would be accepted by the saints at Jerusalem (Rom. 15:30–33). Luke's report of his arrival in Jerusalem reveals why (Acts 21:20f). Rumors were being circulated among Jewish believers

Note continued on next page

LESSON 8

The Corinthians had made a beginning "a year ago" (2 Cor. 8:10). Paul's initial directive to them is found at First Cor. 16:1–2. They had made a good beginning, but now Paul must urge them to complete the work (2 Cor. 8:10f; 9:1–5), their tardiness perhaps being due to the influence of Paul's critics among them (cf. 11:7–15; 12:13–17). Second Corinthians 7:16 is, therefore, important background to Chapters 8 & 9. Had Paul not felt "good courage concerning" the Corinthians in everything, I doubt that he would have been able to proceed with the collection of money among them.

As it is, no other passage has as much to teach us about giving—how to give and how to move other Christians to give. This is the place to which we must return again and again to keep our minds straight on this subject.

Macedonian Zeal Used to Motivate the Corinthians (8:1–15)

Paul had previously boasted to the Macedonian Christians about the good beginning that had been made among the Achaians, and the zeal of the latter had stirred the Macedonians to action (9:1f). What a turnabout! Now Paul uses the zeal of the Macedonians to motivate the Corinthians to complete the job.

God's Grace in Macedonia (1–5)

1. Paul's report about Macedonia is expressed in a perhaps unexpected manner. What did Paul make known to the Corinthians? (1).[2]

---

that Paul was not faithful to the Mosaic tradition. Had that story been widely accepted among Jewish Christians, the church would likely have split. The Gentile churches planted by Paul would not have been recognized by the Jewish churches. That is the reason for Paul's conciliatory actions (Acts 21:22–26). They were intended to lay the rumors to rest, and like the collection itself, to cement the two groups together. God's purpose was not to establish two churches, a Jewish church and a Gentile church, but only one—one body in which Jews and Gentiles would be united in Christ. The epistle to the Ephesians deals with this subject, and should be understood with Paul's struggles and the price he was willing to pay for the unity of the body in the background.

[2] God's grace given in the churches of Macedonia (1), manifested in their gift (2–5). (The same Greek construction is used in 16.) Surprisingly, it is not: "how much

Note continued on next page

2 CORINTHIANS CHAPTER 8

2. *Explanation of this grace given in the Macedonian churches (2).*
    a. What was the condition that was present in Macedonia as they gave?[3]
    b. What two remarkable characteristics were present in Macedonia?[4]
    c. These two characteristics were productive of wealth. In what way?[5]
3. *Four characteristics of Macedonian giving (3–5):*
    a. What is suggested by "beyond their power"? (3).
    b. What about "of their own accord"? (3).[6]

Macedonia has given for Jerusalem"; nor: "the grace of God given to the Jerusalem saints"; but: God's grace in the churches of Macedonia, their giving being a manifestation of God's grace operative among them (cf. 9:8, 12–15). Giving is not viewed through these chapters as a tax or a burden to bear, but rather, as a blessing of divine grace. Even if one rich person could give enough to meet the church's entire budget, still each person would need to give as he was able. We need the blessing that comes from giving.

[3] *Much proof of affliction*, or "a great trial of affliction"—the type experience that would put a person to the test.

[4] *Deep poverty* is literally poverty down to the depths.

[5] The Greek *haplotes* (liberality) is more than generosity. The word is literally singleness (ASV margin) or simplicity (KJV margin); "*singleness, simplicity, sincerity, mental honesty*; the virtue of one who is free from pretence and dissimulation" (GT, 57b); the opposite of doubleness or duplicity; the mind being fixed on a single thing, the desire for it not being spoiled or contaminated by ulterior thought, motive or purpose. The Macedonians had no mixed feelings or misgivings (cf. 9:7), no doubleness: "We are so poor, somebody else ought to be giving to us." They were rich in single-heartedness. Contr. Matt. 6:1f, 5, 16. Thus the givers were rich. Giving was a manifestation of divine grace.

[6] Grk *authairetos*: "self-chosen; ... voluntary, of free choice, of one's own accord" (GT, 84). Paul did not "wring arms"; there were no efforts to persuade. The Macedonians were told of the beginnings in Achaia (9:2), but evidently not with the intention of putting them under pressure. Paul seems to have felt they would be unable to participate (cf. 8:4).

LESSON 8

    c. If I could use the word paradoxically, speaking "tongue in cheek," I would call their giving "selfish." They wanted something, and they begged Paul and his associates for it. What was it? (4).[7]

    d. Again surprisingly, the only reference to the thing given is verse 5. What did they give?[8]

Challenge to the Corinthians (6–15)

The emphasis remains on the spiritual advantage to the giver. As you study Paul's challenge to the Corinthians, consider whether you think he is looking out for the recipients or the givers.

1. *First the call to share in grace (6–7).*
    a. Titus was to be sent back to Corinth (6).[9] For what purpose this time?
    b. What does Paul mean by "this grace" (twice in 6–7) and what are the implications of this terminology?[10]
2. How does Paul explain his use of the Macedonians as a model? (8).[11]

---

[7] *This grace* is defined by what follows. The opportunity to have a fellowship (joint participation, a share) in the ministering to the saints was seen as a blessing (grace) which they were determined to get.

[8] The Greek word order in the description of what they gave runs thus: "their own selves first to the Lord and to us etc." as agents of his purposes (5). *Not as we had hoped*, for their meager resources would not arouse great expectations. The only indication of the object given is verse 5. Any gift of money was only a reflection of their sacrifice of themselves. Compare the widow (Mark 12:41–44), who in effect put herself into the treasury. Does our giving amount to a gift of self, or is it so meager as not even to be missed? The characteristics of Macedonian giving shows how giving can become a grace (or a gift).

[9] Observe the connection. The Macedonian sacrifice of themselves was the motivation behind Paul's further action.

[10] Observe Paul's desire for the Corinthians to share "this grace." Giving is treated as another grace comparable to other gifts of grace (7; cf. 1 Cor. 1:4–7).

[11] He uses the earnestness (or zeal) of the Macedonians to test the Corinthians' love. The example of others can put us to the test. Leslie Diestelkamp's autobiographical

Note continued on next page

3. Verse 9 gives the reason Paul was able to deal with the Corinthians as he did (8). What explains why he could deal with the Corinthians without giving orders, but instead, moving them by appeal to the Macedonians' example?[12]

4. What was Paul's judgment about what would be to the advantage of the Corinthians? (10–11).[13]

5a. Verse 12 provides an explanation bearing on the idea of giving out of one's ability. What word describes what God wants to see in his people? (12).

5b. That being the case, what is the job of preachers and teachers when it comes to teaching people about giving?[14]

5c. In what way should verse 12 be a great encouragement to poor people?

6. *Elaboration on Giving Out of Ability (13–15).* Paul guards against the misconception that the intention was to impoverish one in order to ease the burden of another. What was his intention instead?

   a. What is meant by "equality" (14)?

   b. How is the idea of "equality" illustrated by the citation of Exodus 16:18 in verse 15?

   c. *Discussion:* The right way of providing against the future; giving as reflecting a Christian's mind with regard to the future and future needs. How do these verses speak to this subject?

Here Am I, Send Me had that effect on me. So does Denny Allan's work in Brazil. Both have made me examine myself. We must pay attention to Paul's method. He did not use orders, setting minimums or twisting arms. God's intention with regard to giving cannot be fulfilled that way. Observe the way Paul works on the heart.

[12] He was dealing with people who knew the grace of Christ—who had experienced that grace. Someone else may call the Macdonians "fools," but not the Corinthians. They understood giving. Christians are not pagans, but disciples of Christ, who have learned about giving at the foot of the cross.

[13] The older versions use the word *expedient*, which means profitable or advantageous. Paul was not just looking out for the welfare of the poor saints in Jerusalem. He was looking out for the Corinthians even more.

[14] To produce the "readiness." Grk *prothumia* is "eagerness" or "inclination."

LESSON 8

Arrangements for Completion of "This Grace" (8:16–24)

The Role of Titus (16–17)

1. Why is thanks given to God? (16).

2. Throughout the chapter emphasis is placed on the attitude of the preachers toward the givers. What is meant by *the same earnest care for you* (16)?[15]

3. How is the earnest care of Titus for the Corinthians illustrated in verse 17? Notice two points in particular:

    a. Explain the exhortation (17a) accepted by Titus (cf. 6).

    b. But Titus did not have to be pressured into taking this job, did he? (17b). What is said about his attitude?[16]

4. *Discussion and Application*: Neither Titus nor the other men mentioned below treat their task as an undesirable assignment. How important is it for the Corinthians to know the attitudes of these men being sent to assist in this task?

    a. What effect would these attitudes likely have on the Corinthians?

    b. What can be learned to guide men with similar responsibilities today? Or perhaps: to guide us in the selection of men for similar responsibilities?

A Second Brother (18–21)

1. Paul discusses two other brothers who would come with Titus without naming them. Perhaps they would be known from the characterizations given. What twofold characterization is given of this second brother? (18f).[17]

---

[15] *The same earnest care for you* looks back to Paul's own attitude toward the Corinthians (10f). Both men had a concern for the good of the giver. Grk *spoude* as in verse 8 with regard to the zeal of the Macedonians.

[16] Grk *spoudaios* (here and in 22) is akin to the word used in 16; it means "active, diligent, zealous, earnest" (GT, 585a). *Of his own accord* (as in 3): Self-chosen, voluntary, of free choice.

[17] Take note! Such a man sent on this mission! *The brother* who had *praise* (or *fame*) *in the gospel through all the churches* is identified with Luke in an early tradition, with implications for the writing and date of the Gospel; but we cannot be quite sure of the identification.

2 CORINTHIANS CHAPTER 8

2. "This grace" (19) again! (cf. 1, 4, 6, 7).[18] What two things did Paul and his associates have in view as they ministered "this grace"? (19).[19]

3. An explanation with regard to the arrangements made (20–21).
   a. What did Paul and his associates want to avoid? (20).[20]

   b. What was the general principle on which they acted? (21; cf. Prov. 3:4 in the Septuagint).

   c. *Discussion*: The importance of appearing right as well as being right.

Description of a Third Brother Sent with Them (22)

1. What experience had Paul and his associates had of this man in the past?

2. What made him even *much more earnest* about the present task?

3. Again Paul gives attention to the attitude of the messengers. How would their attitudes put subtle and gentle pressure on the Corinthians?

Personal Certification of the Men Involved (23)

1. What personal certification does Paul place on Titus?

2. What about the two unnamed brothers?[21]

Demonstration Called For On the Part of the Corinthians (24)

... a display "in the face of the churches" represented by these men. What two points were to be demonstrated?[22]

---

[18] The Greek *charis* is also used in First Cor. 16:3 for the Corinthian gift.

[19] For *the glory of the Lord* cf. 9:12. For *our readiness* cf. 11f. The work was not considered a distasteful chore.

[20] The Grk *hadrotes* means "abundance" and is so translated in KJV; "bounty" in ASV; "generous gift" in NASB; "lavish gift" in NKJB (after AG, 18f).

[21] *Messengers* is from the Greek *apostolos*.

[22] Cf. verse 8 on the first. The second will be explained by 9:1–5.

LESSON 9
Second Corinthians 9

Paul's Glorying on Behalf of the Corinthians (9:1–7)

This passage directly relates to what Paul has just said about glorying on behalf of the Corinthians. He elaborates here, telling them about his boast on behalf of them to the Macedonians. But he also explains the precautions he has taken to make sure neither he and his group nor the Corinthians would be embarrassed by what they found upon their arrival in Corinth.

Paul used the earnestness of the Macedonians to test the sincerity of the Corinthians' love (8:8). But now we see that he certainly did not expect a lack of love to be exposed. In fact, the second half of Chapter 8 has brimmed with confidence in the Corinthians, and his attitude toward them was already set forth at the end of Chapter 7. So rather, Paul really expected the collection to provide an occasion for the love he thought was in them to be put on display (8:24).

Writing to Encourage Ministering to the Saints Superfluous (1–2)
1. How is this passage related to the end of ch. 8?

2a. Paul says "it is superfluous[1] for me to write to you" about "the ministering to the saints" (1). How does he explain this statement? (2a).

2b. What boast had Paul made about them to the Macedonians?

2c. What effect did Corinthian zeal have on the Macedonians?[2]

The Reason for Sending Brothers in Advance (3–5)
1. What was the purpose of sending the brothers in advance? (3–4).

2a. What further explanation of the purpose is made in verse 5?

---

[1] Grk *perissos*: "exceeding the usual number or size" (AG, 651), going beyond what is necessary.

[2] Precisely the effect Paul hoped the Macedonian example would now have on the Corinthians (8:8).

2b. The Greek word *eulogia*, used twice (in 5) for the gift, literally means "blessing." The gift had been called a "grace" (8:19) and now a "blessing." Paul wanted the blessing promised to be ready as a blessing, not as extortion or covetousness. Such a gift could represent either a blessing or covetousness. The Greek for the latter is *pleonexia*, which means "a desire for more"; the greedy desire for more and more for self; the tight grip on one's possessions (cf. Prov. 30:15f). Now a question:

> What would our gifts be like if regarded as blessings bestowed upon the recipients? In other words, if we wanted them to bless the recipients?[3]

2c. *For personal reflection:* Does our giving reflect the desire to bless the recipient? Or does it reflect a greedy, covetous heart?

3. Looking back over 1–5, but especially 3–5, consider: How do these verses reflect a thoughtfulness toward the Corinthians on Paul's part?

Brief Instruction on Individual Attitudes in Giving (6-7)

The "But this" with which verse 6 begins may introduce a contrast not merely with the immediately preceding verse, but with 1–5 as a whole. "It is superfluous" to write to you about ministering to the saints, Paul had written. But he did have these few words about making the collection a blessing rather than a reflection of covetousness (5).

1. Consider Paul's metaphor (6). How is giving like sowing?

2. Observe that the characterization of this "sowing" is closely related to the terms of verse 5. What term from verse 5 might explain sowing that is done "sparingly"?

---

[3] Contrast a miserly employer willing to pay what the contract calls for and not one cent more. He is not out to bless his employees, but to keep as much as he can for himself. Contrast also the payment of a debt: "How much do I owe you?" That is what we mean to pay and not one cent more. We are not out to bless the business, but to get what we want as cheap as we can. Contrast also the way most people pay taxes. We are willing to pay what we owe, but are not anxious to throw in a little more for a government that wastes so much.

LESSON 9

3. On the positive side, the Greek for *bountifully* is literally *on the basis of blessings*.[4] So verse 6 encourages giving that makes the gift a blessing, which is the thing to be desired according to verse 5.

   a. So again: What would giving be like if done "on the basis of blessings"—i. e., perhaps, with the desire to bless the recipient?[5]

   b. What encouragement is given in 6b to sowing on the basis of blessings?[6]

4. Summarize Paul's description of what God wants to see in givers (7a).[7]

5. What reason is given for giving in this manner? (7b).[8]

6. *For reflection*: The whole emphasis is on the heart, not the amount. But suppose someone does not want to give and cannot give with the attitudes called for. What then should be done? Should we try to bring pressures to bear that might force him to give? What can we learn from Paul's approach?[9]

---

[4] The preposition is *epi*, meaning upon; hence referring to the basis or ground of the sowing.

[5] How would that compare, for example, with the way most people approach the paying of income taxes?

[6] The manner of reaping is determined by the manner of sowing.

[7] Each as he has freely chosen (Grk *proaireo*, GT, 537a; AG, 702) in his own heart; "as he has made up his mind" (AG, RSV). Compare the concept *of one's own accord* (in 8:3 &17); the alternative being the result of external pressures causing one to do other than he really desires. *Not out of sorrow, pain* or *grief* (literally); i. e. "with a sour, reluctant mind" (GT on Grk *lupe*, 383b; cf. AG, 482a), leaving one sorry he gave, wishing he did not have to give. *Or out of necessity* or *compulsion* (Grk *anagke*, GT, 36b; AG, 52)—some sort of pressure moving one to do other than he would wish.

[8] "God loves a joyful, glad, cheerful giver" (Grk *hilaros*); one glad to give; glad he gave; wishing he could give more; one who gives joyfully.

[9] We should never abandon Paul's methods, which is to say: We should never try to pressure people into giving. But people who do not want to give may not be

Note continued on next page

2 CORINTHIANS CHAPTER 9

The Divine Enabler Behind the Collection (9:8–11)

From the statement about the giver God loves (7) to the end of the chapter the entire focus is upon God. Trust in the God who can be described as he is in verses 8–11 is a key to cheerful giving. For how can one give joyfully if he is eaten up with anxiety over his own needs?

What God Can Do (8–9)

1. What is God able to do, according to 8a?[10]

2a. What is the aim or purpose of this abundance of grace? (8b).[11]

2b. Explain the reference to *every good work* by drawing upon the overall context of Chapters 8 & 9, and also the quotation that immediately follows.

3. How is this assurance illustrated by the quotation (in 9)?[12]

What God Will Do (10–11)

1a. Consider why God is described as he is in verse 10.

1b. What will this One *who supplies seed to the sower*, etc. do for the Corinthian Christians?

2a. In what way will they be made rich? (11).[13]

2b. To what would their singleheartedness (in giving) give rise?

---

ready for a lesson on giving money. What is needed, instead, is a meditation at the foot of the cross. Paul could deal with the Corinthians as he did because they knew the grace of Christ (cf. 8:9). If that does not work, give it up!

[10] *All grace* refers to gifts of all kinds, whatever is needed. Cf. 8:1 for an example illustrating what is said in verses 8–9.

[11] Not that God will make us rich necessarily. The Macedonians were poor, but able to do what is said here.

[12] Consider Ps. 112:9 in context. "He" is not God, but the man who fears God.

[13] *For all singleness*, a more literal translation of the Greek *haplotes*, which is used in 8:2 and explained in a footnote at that place. The Macedonians are an example of what is said here.

LESSON 9

Elucidation of This Praise to God: The Anticipated Effect of the Collection (9:12–15)

Twofold Effect of "The Ministration of This Service" (12)

What two effects of the collection are anticipated?

The Surprising Grounds of Praise (13)

1. First the occasion of praise: What is meant by *the proving of this ministration*?[14]

2. Then the surprising grounds of the praise that results from this ministry. The recipients are anticipated as glorifying God, but not for the money they have received; rather, for two things which the testing of this ministration has revealed about the givers. What are the two grounds upon which the recipients glorify God?[15]

---

[14] This language has been used before in connection with the collection (8:8, 24). This ministry would test and prove something about the Corinthians.

[15] The preposition is *epi*, upon; hence *two grounds upon which* they glorify God. *The obedience of your confession to the gospel of Christ* is a reference to the reality and genuineness of their conversion. Their confession was not just hollow words, but characterized by obedience. Many of the Jews must have found it hard to believe anything good could come of the conversion of these formerly idolatrous and immoral Gentiles. But the testing through which they were put by the collection proved that they were not just pretending; they were for real. Their response to the opportunity gave evidence of the obedience which ought to characterize one's confession or profession of the truth of the gospel.

The other ground of praise is *the singleness of your fellowship to them and to all*, a more exact translation. Grk *haplotes* is the word already used twice for singleness (8:2; 9:11). See 8:2 for explanation. It means singleness as opposed to doubleness or duplicity. The word often translated contribution or distribution is *koinonia*, the usual Greek word for fellowship. The contribution was not to all, but only to the poor saints in Jerusalem (Rom. 15:25–27; 1 Cor. 16:3). Paul is speaking of the sincere fellowship which the Corinthians manifested toward them (the saints who received the relief, according to verse 12) and toward all the saints, wherever they were. *The singleness of this fellowship*, which amounts to a genuine recognition

Note continued on next page

2 CORINTHIANS CHAPTER 9

Reciprocation of Brotherly Feeling by the Jerusalem Saints (14)

The recipients of the relief are anticipated not only as glorifying God for the reasons cited in verse 13, but also as reciprocating the brotherly feeling manifested toward them by the givers: *by means of their petition on your behalf longing for you.* But what is the reason for their longing?[16]

Closing Thanksgiving (15)

1. After verse 14, what must be God's "indescribable gift"?[17]
2. What are the implications of the word "unspeakable" or "indescribable"?

---

of these other saints as brothers, was manifested by means of the testing of this ministration. The poor saints at Jerusalem are anticipated as recognizing it and praising God for it.

Plainly, Paul's plan for this great collection was more than simple relief of needy people. He hoped it would serve to strengthen the bonds of unity between Jews and Gentiles in the one body. See further the introduction to this section.

[16] Again, the reason may be a bit surprising. It goes deeper than the gift to *the surpassing grace of God upon you*, which they understand to lie behind the gift and to explain it. Thus Paul's treatment of the collection begins and ends on the same note. Like the giving of the Macedonians (8:1–2), the giving of the Corinthians (9:14) is seen as reflecting the operations of divine grace in them. Do you want to teach people to give? Then do not come at it from a legalistic standpoint. Teach them about the grace of God. They will not need a commandment when they "know the grace of our Lord Jesus Christ" (8:8–9).

[17] The indescribable grace bestowed in Christ (8:9) and now manifested by the collection (8:1, 6–7; 9:8, 14).

PART THREE

Vindication

of Paul's Apostleship

Against False Teachers

SECOND CORINTHIANS **10–13**

LESSON 10
Second Corinthians 10

Introduction to Chapters 10–13

Paul had established the church at Corinth, and continued to have a deep interest in and relationship with it. But false teachers, Judaizers (cf. 11: 18–22), had come to Corinth and tried to undermine Paul's influence and teaching by personal attacks upon his integrity and his apostleship. He has alluded to them before (1:17; 3:1; 5:12; 6:14–7:1); but now his entire attention is focused on their attack. Part Three is his answer to them, though he does not address them directly. He addresses the Corinthian saints with reference to them.

The issue was more than personality—an attitude toward Paul personally. His apostleship was at stake, and with it, the truth of the gospel and the salvation of the church. More than self-defense (cf. 12:19), Part Three is an effort to save the church from the destructive influence of unscrupulous false teachers.

INTRODUCTORY WARNINGS, CHALLENGES AND EXPLANATIONS
SECOND COR. 10

Paul's Request of the Corinthians and the Threat of Vengeance Against Rebellion (10:1–6)

Paul exhorts (1), even begs (2) the Corinthians: "Do not force me to turn my powerful spiritual weapons against you." He knew he would have "to be bold against" the false teachers when he came to Corinth, but hoped he would not have to treat the disciples as he did his opponents. This letter is an effort to separate the disciples from these teachers, so he would not have to come down hard on them as he would these teachers (2). So we incidentally learn something about the purpose of the epistle, and especially this section (cf. 13:10).

Paul continues with military imagery, and speaks of the powerful spiritual weapons that were at his disposal (3–6). It would not be wise to

LESSON 10

challenge Paul, his authority and his weapons. His weapons are too strong. He warns the Corinthian Christians, indeed begs them: Do not let it come to a test. Do not side with the false teachers and have these weapons turned against you as well.

1a. In previous parts of the epistle Paul often associated himself with his coworkers by the use of "we" and "us," but this section begins *I Paul myself* (1). What could account for this unusual emphasis?[1]

1b. By what means (Grk *dia*) does Paul make his entreaty or exhortation? (1; cf. Matt. 11:29b).

1c. How would you explain Paul's self-description in the last half of verse 1, in light of verse 10?[2]

2a. What is Paul's plea to the Corinthians? In other words, what did he not want to have to do when he was present in Corinth? (2).

2b. What two groups ("you" and "some") are distinguished in verse 2?[3]

2c. What miscalculation were Paul's opponents making about him and his coworkers? (2).[4]

---

[1] The plural is used some, even in this chapter. But the singular is frequent in Chapters 10–13. Undoubtedly the attack was primarily against Paul and only incidentally against his associates. But more was involved. The emphasis places the full weight of Paul's personality against his opponents and their slander. "I Paul myself"—the very one so slandered among you (cf. 1b with 10)—beg you not to make me show my courage among you (2).

[2] It is not Paul's description of his behavior and bearing, but uses the words of his opponents (10), who said he was strong at a distance, but weak when present, perhaps even intimating he was afraid to come to Corinth. His use of "the meekness and gentleness of Christ" may have given these men a plausible basis for this slander. The contrast with their overbearing manner (11:20), which shows their notion of a teacher, also helps to define their criticism of Paul.

[3] He counted on showing courage and boldness against *some*, the false teachers, in a personal confrontation; but begs this church planted by him not to side with the false teachers and also come to know his courage.

[4] *According to the flesh* i. e., the ordinary human way, which is weak and even sinful. The walk of one who would be bold while writing letters from a distance, but lowly and humble when present (cf. 1, 10).

3. What reason is given (in 3) for Paul's plea (in 2)? In other words, why does he beg them not to put his courage to the test?[5]

4. Paul elaborates his assertion with regard to methods of warfare (4). What does he say about the power of the weapons used by him and his colleagues?[6]

5a. Verses 5 & 6 continue the description of the waging of war, but partly replacing the imagery with literal reality. For example, how are "strongholds" (or fortresses) explained in 5?[7]

---

[5] The reason is this miscalculation of his opponents. The case is not as they regard it. We do not make war as they think we do. We have mighty weapons at our disposal. In effect Paul is warning the Corinthians that they must beware coming up against such weapons. That is why he begs them not to put his courage to the test. True, in ourselves we are but weak men, who *walk in the flesh*, but *we do not make war according to the flesh*, which is the great miscalculation of his opponents. In ordinary conflict with human means of warfare—slander and misrepresentation, for example, such as Paul's opponents used—they could easily excel. But Paul had weapons not understood by them.

[6] *Of the flesh*, again with implications of weakness (cf. Is. 30:1–5; 31:1–3). *Mighty before God*, i. e. mighty indeed! Grk *ochuroma* (strongholds), "a castle, stronghold, fortress, fastness," is used metaphorically of "anything on which one relies" (cf. the Septuagint in Prov. 10:29 & 21:22); "in 2 Co. 10:4 of the arguments and reasonings by which a disputant endeavors to fortify his opinion and defend it against his opponent" (GT, 471); "the (subtle) reasonings (of opponents) likened to fortresses" (GT on *kathaireo*, 312). *Casting down* is "to destroy *logismoi*, sophistries, and everything that opposes the knowledge of God" (AG, 601a). So v. 5. Paul is comparing spiritual weapons to powerful war machines such as a battering ram, machinery which could overthrow a great fort.

[7] *Imaginations*, or *reasonings* (Grk *logismos*), here "such as is hostile to the Christian faith" (GT, 380a); "calculation, reasoning, reflection, thought," here: "sophistries" (AG, 476f). Reference to the various human philosophies and systems of thought; speculations. "Logismoi here = the reasonings or rationalizations of self-centred man" (Hughes). Such are the strongholds in which men take refuge. Grk *hupsoma* (high thing): *"thing elevated, height ... specifically elevated structure i. e. barrier, rampart, bulwark:* 2 Co. 10:5" (GT, 647a). For example, a fort built on a height. Again with reference to the reasonings of men; the systems of thought erected against the knowledge of God (cf. AG on *epairo*, 281f, and on *hupsoma*, 851b); to prevent God from being known.

LESSON 10

5b. The imagery is continued by reference to war captives being taken. How is this part of the imagery applied?[8]

5c. What additional feature of this military imagery is applied in verse 6?[9]

5d. When, according to the last clause of verse 6, would such punishment of disobedience take place?[10]

---

[8] The hostile thoughts or evil purposes (Grk *noema*, used for "devices" of Satan in 2:11) are conquered, defeated; their power broken, they are taken captive, replaced by subjection and submission to Christ. The idea is that "whoever is devising evil against Christ is caused to desist from his purpose and submit himself to Christ (as Paul sets him forth)" (GT, 427a). "We take captive every design to make it obedient to Christ" (AG, 540b). "We take every thought captive and make it obey Christ" (AG on *aichmalotizo*, 27a). "In this way the genuine Christian position is established. The rebellion of the human heart is quelled, the truth of God prevails, and the divine sovereignty is acknowledged" (Hughes). "There are no more devisings of our own thinking. They are put into chains, dragged away, executed. Now there is only listening with hearts and thoughts that are completely obedient only to Christ" (Lenski).

[9] Paul and his companions are portrayed as standing in a state of readiness to punish (so GT, 193b and AG, 238b on the Grk *ekdikeo* here and in Rev. 6:10 & 19:2) all disobedience. Grk *ekdikeo* used here "of the Apostle's readiness to use his apostolic authority in punishing disobedience on the part of his readers" (VED). Compare a Roman garrison set up in conquered territory to take quick action against the least sign of revolt. "Moffatt suggestively treats this verse as a continuation of the military metaphors of the preceding verses, ...: 'I am prepared to court-martial anyone who remains insubordinate, once your submission is complete.' As apostolic commander of the Christian forces at Corinth, Paul is now holding himself in readiness to arraign and punish every case of disobedience and treachery" (Hughes). With regard to this punishment of rebellion, compare the process that is threatened in 13:1f and also the judgment that was called for in the case of the incestuous man (1 Cor. 5:3–5, 12f).

[10] *When your obedience shall be made full* explains why Paul does not rush right down on the Corinthian disciples, meting out quick justice. He was giving them opportunity to correct the situation and complete their obedience, thus avoiding being caught up in the justice meted out to false teachers. Again we have indication of the purpose of this epistle (cf. 12:19–21; 13:7–10).

Introduction to Paul's Defense:
Appeal to Undeniable Facts (10:7–18)

Paul's authority, and perhaps even his status as a Christian, had been challenged by false teachers. His answer to the challenge seems to have been determined by the way his position was being undermined by these teachers.

How can he meet such a challenge? Where can he start? Why not with the facts that stare the Corinthians right in the face? Paul was a Christian, it must be conceded, and even more: He had the authority of an apostle, as his coming appearance in Corinth would manifest. If his opponents lingered there, they would soon find it out. They had better count on his being just as strong in person as in his letters. Any other view would be a complete miscalculation.

Challenge Issued by Paul (7a)

Three different constructions of this statement are grammatically possible:

(1) The verb could be an indicative (statement of fact) as in the ASV text: "You look at the things that are before your face."

(2) The sentence could be punctuated as a question: "Do you look at the things that are before your face?" (ASV margin; KJV).

(3) The verb could be an imperative (command) form: "Look at the things that are before your face!" So RSV, NEB, NASB margin, NIV margin ("the obvious facts") & Phillips ("things which stare you in the face").

Since context must determine the correct construction, which view best fits the context? Does 7b seem to elaborate a mistaken view being taken in Corinth (a superficial view based on appearances), or is it more likely to be an elaboration of a challenge to look at "the obvious facts"?[11]

---

[11] Certainly the latter, in my opinion. "Paul points to what is right before everybody's eyes and lets the simple, obvious, undeniable facts tell the Corinthians what the Corinthians should have seen all along" (Lenski). "... 'Look at what is before your eyes'—that is, 'Face the obvious facts', the facts so well known to them regarding Paul and his apostleship" (Hughes). See also C. K. Barrett and F. F. Bruce. Compare 12:6b where Paul says he passed up an attempt to make his case on the basis of "visions and revelations" that would be beyond the ability of any man to examine, "lest any man should account of me above that which he sees me *to be*, or hears from me."

Starting Point of a Defense: Paul and Associates Undeniably Christians as Any Real Christian Would Recognize (7b)

What conclusion would "any man" have to reach about Paul, if he simply reasoned over "the obvious facts" of the case? (7b).[12]

Another Claim That Will Stand: The Authority of an Apostle (8–11)

1a. Paul has made one claim (7b). But he could glory "somewhat more" (KJV), "somewhat further" (NASB) or "more abundantly" (NASB margin). What additional claim could he make? (8).

1b. What was the source of apostolic authority? (8).[13]

1c. What was its purpose? (8).[14]

---

[12] Paul is not referring to false teachers, whom he did not regard as Christians (11:3f, 12–15), but to "any man" among the Corinthian disciples who had confidence that he belonged to Christ, and proposing a test which any Christian among them could make. It is based on the obvious facts that stare them right in the face. The test resembles the one proposed in First Cor. 14:37. Any man who claimed to be a prophet or spiritual (led of the Spirit) would certainly be able to recognize that the things Paul wrote were the commandment of the Lord. So here. "If any man trusts in himself that he is Christ's," all he needs to do is use his mind again ("consider," Grk *logizomai*) and he will recognize "that, even as he is Christ's, so also are we."

How did they come to trust in themselves that they were Christ's? How did they become Christians? Paul was the one who had brought them to faith (cf. 1 Cor. 3:5b) and made them Christians in the first place. So all they needed to do was to reason a little bit. Did they consider themselves to be Christians? Then let them think again and they would recognize that Paul was a Christian too. That at least provided a place to begin dealing with this problem caused by the false teachers. But Paul had every right to claim even more (8).

[13] Since apostolic authority was not a human accomplishment, but something received as a gift from the Lord (cf. 1 Cor. 4:7), Paul's claims with regard to authority were not inconsistent with the rule set forth in verse 17.

[14] *For building you up, and not for casting you down.* The last verb is the same word used in verse 4. Though it was sometimes necessary to use his power for "casting down," the real purpose of it was "building you up," and Paul did not want to have to use it for "casting down" (cf. 13:10).

1d. What would be the result should he make this additional claim? (8).[15]
2. The purpose clause *that I may not seem etc.* (9), and including the elaboration that follows in verses 10 & 11, is directly connected with the statement at the end of verse 8: *I shall not be put to shame.* He would not turn out to be one who only terrified people by letters at a safe distance (9), as his critics claimed (10), but rather as described (in 11).
   a. What did Paul's critics in Corinth say about him? (10).
   b. Better not count on it! says Paul (11). What should they expect instead?

The Plain Facts Concerning Paul's Relation to Corinth (12–16)[16]
1. How would you explain the link between 12 and the preceding verses?[17]

---

[15] *I shall not be put to shame.* Even this claim would not be exposed as groundless, but rather be supported by the plain facts that stared the Corinthians in the face (7a). Paul would be found to be exactly what he claimed to be.

[16] The plural used throughout these verses no doubt includes Paul's associates. The justification of the heading as a whole will appear as one works his way through the thought of these verses. It will also be obvious that his explanations are a response to the false teachers who have come to Corinth.

[17] Verses 8–11 are a tightly woven unit. Paul has said that though he should glory about his authority he would not be put to shame, with his claim exposed as groundless. His elaboration amounts to this: It is not as his opponents say, that he was a terror by letter from a safe distance, but only a weakling and certainly nothing to be feared when present. He says they should count on the fact that his deeds when present will harmonize perfectly with his letters from afar.

He continues now with the explanation: For we are not like our boastful opponents who commend themselves. They use no true measuring rod, but only measure themselves by themselves. No real measuring having been done, they are left "without understanding," entirely under an illusion about themselves. Were we like them, we might be put to shame when we appear in Corinth, the deeds when present not at all justifying the claims from afar.

LESSON 10

2a. With what class of men does Paul say he and his colleagues did not dare include himself among? (12).[18]

2b. By what standard do these men measure themselves, so as to commend themselves?[19]

---

[18] *We do not dare* (KJV, NIV) is from the same verb used in 2. Grk *tolmao*: "dare, have the courage, be brave enough," perhaps here, something like "bring oneself" or "presume" (AG, 821b; cf. GT, 627b). We shrink from; we do not have the courage or boldness to do this thing. What they shrink from is defined by infinitives. The first, from *egkrino*, combines *eg* (= *en*, in) with *krino* (to judge); hence "to reckon among, judge among: *tina tini*, to judge one worthy of being admitted to a certain class"—only here in NT (GT, 167a); "to class *tina tini* someone with someone" (AG, 216b); "of the Apostle's dissociation of himself and his fellow-missionaries from those who commended themselves" (VED, "Number"). The other, from *sugkrino*, combines *sug* (= *sun*, with) with *krino*; hence *to judge with, to compare* (GT, 593b; AG, 774b). So altogether the play on words amounts to this: We do not dare, simply would not have the courage to put ourselves in the same class with or to compare ourselves with such men. We count on being bold (2); but we are not that bold. Obviously the language drips with sarcasm—maybe the only way to deal with such arrogance.

Certain of them that commend themselves. The class these men belong to. They come highly recommended ... by themselves. Compare 11:20 for the "brass" of these men. We do not have that much boldness, says Paul. We would be afraid of being put to shame (8), i. e., having the hollowness of our claims exposed. Amazing! that such men had the brass to accuse Paul of doing the very thing of which they themselves were guilty (3:1). Paul has already responded that he and his companions only commended themselves in a certain way (4:2; 6:4) and for a certain unselfish purpose (5:12f). How ashamed this analysis must have made the Corinthians feel! to have lent an ear to attacks on Paul from such men, on the ground of their own self-recommendation.

[19]*Measuring themselves by themselves.* GT, 407b (on *metreo*) explains the Greek: "to measure one's self by one's self, to derive from one's self the standard by which one estimates one's self." Imagine a boy standing against a wall and making a mark at the top of his head. He steps away for a moment, then comes back to the wall and stands up against it, exclaiming: "My! How tall I am! I come right up to the mark!"

Note continued on next page

2c. How does Paul characterize those who so measure themselves?[20]

3. In contrast to such men, how does Paul explain the standard according to which his claims (i. e., glorying) are made? (13).[21]

> His excitement is silly, of course. He has used no real standard of measurement at all, and has done no real measuring. He has only deceived himself.
>
> Then imagine preachers denigrating others who do not "hew to the line" as they do, setting themselves up as the standard of measurement. Everyone else is measured against that standard, and naturally comes up short. Of course they themselves grade out 100%, coming right up to the mark. And no wonder! for they were the mark. Such absurdity is no real measuring at all.
>
> Finally, consider one claiming to be a Christian on the basis of a certain experience he has had. He is asked: "How do you know that experience makes one a Christian?" and replies: "Because it is my experience; and I know I am a Christian."
>
> [20] They *are without understanding.* Of course! for they have not done any real measuring at all. They only use themselves as the measuring rod, and no real objective measure at all. So they end up under an illusion about themselves.
>
> [21] *Not ... beyond measure,* literally "unto the things without measure" (Grk *eis ta ametra*)—"referring to the sphere Divinely appointed for the Apostle as to his Gospel ministry" (VED, "Measure"), as indicated by the last clause. Our glorying, says Paul, will not exceed a certain measure; it will not operate in the realm of what is unmeasured, perhaps even unmeasurable, like that of his opponents.
>
> *But according to the measure of the measuring rod* (literal meaning of *kanon*) etc. Paul was determined that his glorying would not exceed the realm of things measured. It would be according to the measure of the measuring rod ...
>
> *Which God apportioned to us as a measure.* Cf. Rom. 12:3 where Paul points out that God has dealt every man a measure (Grk *metron*) within which his faith is to operate. Paul himself was given such a measure as a gift of grace. His special gift was that of apostleship (Rom. 1:5). God's measuring rod thus determined the measure within which Paul would act. "He thus has a canon or standard for his work and for the associated claim to apostolic validity which he has not conferred on himself but received from God" (TDNT, III, 599).
>
> *To reach even unto you.* Paul was operating within the sphere God had measured to him when he came to Corinth. Along with Rom. 12:3, Rom. 15:20 & Gal. 2:9 help to define the idea of *measure* as used here; the particular sphere in which Paul's apostleship would be exercised. First Thess. 2:19f, where Paul calls the Thessalonians his "crown of glorying," is also helpful.

LESSON 10

4. When Paul claimed that his assigned sphere of labor reached Corinth, he was not exaggerating (14). What proved as much?[22]

5. So with regard to his claim about Corinth, he was not glorying beyond the measure assigned to him (15a). How is this *glorying beyond measure* further defined in verse 15a?[23]

6. But Paul did not even consider that his divinely apportioned sphere of activity ended at Corinth or with any of the labors he had done so far (15b–16). What hope did he entertain?[24]

---

[22] He and his companions had actually come to Corinth (14b). In fact the Grk *phthano* has the significance pointed out in ASV margin: came before, preceded, anticipated, came first unto you (cf. GT, 652; AG, 856b). The past tense presents the plain historical fact which supports what Paul has said about the Corinthians being included in the realm of activity assigned to him by God. Paul was the one who had planted this work; not his critics, who had come along behind, invading, even trying to steal the work of another (15). The Corinthians were Paul's work (1 Cor. 9:1). He had come to Corinth pursuant of the task assigned to him by God. Is it not so? Who could deny it? What did his critics have to boast about? Paul is presenting the plain, undeniable facts of the case as they stared the Corinthians in the face (7a).

[23] He was not glorying over the work of other men.

[24] *As your faith grows.* The future depended on them. Paul could not leave the areas of his labors in the East until he was confident of the stability of the faith of those left behind. He could not leave a church unsettled. He had hope that Corinth would be so established that he could go on to other work without anxiety. But he could not do so if they continued to tolerate false teachers among them and show themselves so unstable.

What a hindrance immaturity and instability is to the progress of the gospel in the world! Consider what this passage contributes toward the understanding of apostolic strategy. Churches must get stabilized to the point preachers can go on to other fields. They cannot forever need a caretaker to baby them. They must grow up. The object is to get the gospel preached everywhere in the world.

We shall be magnified in you etc. Grk *megaluno* is to make large or great (GT, 394a; AG, 497a)—here "in a figure" meaning "that Paul's apostolic efficiency among the Corinthians may increase more and more and have more abundant results" (GT); thus

Note continued on next page

7. Even as Paul had plans to go to new fields, what was he determined not to do? (16).²⁵

The Only Appropriate Glorying (17–18)

Paul closes out this introduction to his defense against the attacks of false teachers by laying down a general rule with regard to glorying.

1. What is the rule laid down by Paul (in words from Jeremiah 9:24) with regard to glorying? (17).²⁶

"*becoming capable* for further extended working, *the being put into a position for it*," hence the aim stated in v. 16 (Meyer).

This passage, along with Romans 15:20f, is of particular importance as explaining Paul's understanding of his work—the plan or strategy of it.

²⁵ What Paul would not boast about had regard to *ta hetoima* (things ready). Paul is referring to "*what has been accomplished* (by someone else)" (AG on *hetoimos*, 316b); "the things (made) ready (in advance by others), i. e. the Christian churches already founded by them" (GT, 255b); "work already done in another's field" (RSV); "what has been accomplished in the sphere of another" (NASB); "work already done" (NEB & NIV; cf. Phillips). See Romans 15:20f for more light on this matter. Paul would never do what his opponents had done. They had not done the hard work of planting the gospel in a new field, but had come to a church already established and were trying to take possession of a church planted by others. Corinth was not their work but Paul's (1 Cor. 9:1; cf. 2 Cor. 3:1–3). They were trying to steal his work.

²⁶ Paul's integrity and his apostleship had been attacked at Corinth by unscrupulous false teachers trying to steal a work that was not theirs (cf. 14–16). "Are not you my work in the Lord?" Paul had asked (1 Cor. 9:1). With the truth of the gospel and the salvation of this church at stake, Paul had no choice. He was compelled to assert his own claims, i. e. to glory (cf. 12:11). Yet he knew he was treading dangerous ground. He had to set forth his claims in terms that could not be misunderstood or misconstrued, especially with unscrupulous opponents looking for something in him they could turn against him (cf. 1:17; 10:10; 11:10–15; 12:14–18). In these circumstances he draws upon Jeremiah 9:24 to set forth a rule which defines and governs any necessary glorying.

Paul has said he would not glory *beyond measure*, meaning *in other men's labors* (15a) and as glorying in the sphere of another's labor respecting *things*

Note continued on next page

2. What reason is assigned for taking this position—that is, for insisting that glorying must be "in the Lord"? (18)[27]

ready—i. e., things already accomplished by someone else (16). That is what his opponents in Corinth were doing. In their effort to take the church from Paul they were laying claim to another man's work (cf. 1 Cor. 9:1).

One might imagine that any appropriate glorying would be a glorying in one's own accomplishments. Not so. The only appropriate glorying, as defined in a concept drawn from Jeremiah 9:24, is to glory *in the Lord*. The context of Jeremiah 9:24 provides some help with this concept. But Paul's usage is even more helpful. When he first cites this principle in First Cor. 1:31 it is to say that one should not glory in his own achievements, but in the Lord's (cf. Gal. 6:17), which is also what Paul is doing when he asserts his claims in Second Corinthians. He lays claim to authority which was a gift from the Lord (10:8) and glories *not beyond meaure, but according to the measure of the measuring rod which God apportioned to us as a measure* (10:13). But what finally will his glorying amount to? "If I must needs glory," he says, and it was necessary (cf. 12:11), "I will glory of the things that concern my weakness" (11: 30). By so doing he magnified the power of the Lord. For only divine power could explain his accomplishments (cf. 12:8-10; cf. 4:7). They could not possibly be explained as due to the weak human instrument used by the Lord.

Romans 15:14-21 expounds the same concept. "I have therefore my glorying in Christ Jesus in things pertaining to God. For I will not dare to speak of any things save those which Christ worked through me ...," says Paul, elaborating in what immediately follows.

Add, finally, Paul's reports, rehearsing what God has done with him (Acts 14:27; 15:12; 21:19) and leading people to glorify God for what he had accomplished through Paul's ministry rather than to credit the human instrument used by him (Acts 21:20a).

[27] If a man is pleased with himself and commends himself, what is the worth of that? The one approved by God will not be the one who commends himself, but the one commended by the Lord (18; cf. Matt. 25:21a, 23a; 1 Cor. 4:1-5). Grk *sunistemi* (commends) is of frequent occurrence in this epistle (3:1; 4:2; 5:12; 6:4; 7:11; 10:12, 18 twice; 12:11). Grk *dokimos* (approved) means tested and found true, "tried and true, genuine" (AG, 203a; cf. GT, 155a). Compare especially the occurrences in 13:7 & First Cor. 11:19. The word also appears at Romans 14:18 & 16:10, where "the approved one in Christ = *the tried and true Christian*" (AG); 2 Tim. 2:15 & James 1:12. At Second Cor. 13:7 the opposite of "approved" (Grk *dokimos*) is "reprobate" (Grk *adokimos*).

LESSON 11
Second Corinthians 11

"A LITTLE FOOLISHNESS": PAUL'S GLORYING
SECOND COR. 11:1–12:13

Paul continues to vindicate his apostolic ministry against the attacks of false teachers in Corinth. The subject of glorying or boasting has already been introduced (10:8, 13, 15, 17). The Corinthians' toleration of false teachers, who were attempting to undermine Paul's work and to take the church from him, made it necessary for Paul to assert his claims. The truth of the gospel and the salvation of the church were at stake. But Paul was reluctant and embarrassed to have to engage in such boasting. He starts into the matter with a plea that the Corinthians would indulge him "in a little foolishness" (11:1). First he explains why it is necessary (11:2–15); then he sets forth his boast, but in a most surprising manner, boasting in such fashion that credit is heaped upon the Lord Jesus Christ rather than upon himself (11:16–12:13).

Plea for Toleration of "Foolishness" Supported by Explanation of the Reasons for It (11:1–15)

Plea for Toleration of "Foolishness" (1)

1. What is the "foolishness" (or "folly") of which Paul speaks? (Observe that the entire section 11:1–12:13 deals with the subject, but see especially 11:16–21 for a quick answer.)[1]

2. What are the implications of "bear with me"?

---

[1] Paul begins with a wish (Grk *ophelon*) that they would bear with him, but strengthens his expression then with an imperative: *but more (kai) do bear with me*. The Greek verb form could be indicative (*you do bear*); but in my opinion only the imperative fits the context, in which Paul makes it plain in what follows how imperative it is that they bear with him. The Grk *anecho* means to bear, endure, or put up with.

LESSON 11

The Plea (of 1) Supported by Reasons (2–6)

1. *Jealousy Over the Corinthians (2–3).*
   a. How does Paul explain his attitude toward the church? (2a).[2]
   b. Paul's attitude is further explained in 2b-3. How does he explain his role with reference to the Corinthians? (2b).[3]
   c. What did he fear? (3).[4]
   d. What are the implications of "simplicity" (3), especially in reference to the marriage imagery?[5]

---

[2] Grk *zeloo* (I am jealous) is *"to burn with zeal ... (with personal object as here) to desire one earnestly, to strive after, busy one's self about* him" (GT, 271); here "in a good sense *strive, desire, exert oneself earnestly* ... with a personal object *tina be deeply concerned about someone, court someone's favor*" (AG, 338). A godly jealousy is literally *a jealousy of God*; the Grk *zelos* here with a genitive of quality, "a zeal like that of God" (AG, 337b); but others call it a genitive of the subject: "with a jealousy such as God has, hence most pure and solicitous for their salvation" (GT, 271a); not mere human passion and not mere personal offense that the Corinthians might prefer another teacher. See Is. 54:5; 62:5; Jer. 3:1–3; Ezek. 16; Hos. 2:18–20 for God as the husband of his people, a jealous lover who does not tolerate rivals.

[3] Grk *harmozo* is here used of the father's role in the betrothal of a bride: "to betroth, to give one in marriage to any one" (GT, 74a; cf. AG, 107b). Paul had played the father's role (cf. 1 Cor. 4:14f) in the betrothal of the Corinthians to Christ, with the responsibility to protect the purity of the bride until the marriage has been consummated.

[4] Grk *exapatao* (beguiled): to deceive, cheat, lead astray (AG, 273; GT, 221). Grk *panourgia* (craftiness) is the word explained at 4:2. Grk *phtheiro* (be corrupted): *destroy, ruin, corrupt, spoil*; here with reference to the seduction of a virgin (AG, 857); "to be so corrupted as to fall away from a thing" (GT, 652). For simplicity, see the next note.

[5] "Simple" is the opposite of double or complex; "simplicity," the opposite of duplicity. Greek *haplotes* is also at 8:2 & 9:11, 13 with reference to the collection: singleness as opposed to duplicity; mental honesty; here *toward Christ*: "sincere devotion to Christ" (AG, 85f); "sincerity of mind towards Christ, i. e. single-hearted faith in Christ, as opposed to false wisdom in matters pertaining to Christianity" (GT, 57b); singleminded devotion to one husband.

2. **Well to heed Paul's plea if another (and different) Jesus/Spirit/ Gospel is brought (4).**

   a. What was the specific danger threatening the Corinthians, which made necessary Paul's self-vindication? (4 and the following context through 15).

   b. Of two different views of the last clause of verse 4 (summarized below), which best fits the context?

   (1) Most scholarly opinion (and versions) supports the view in the ASV: "you do well to bear with *him*," usually understanding the statement as sarcastic: "You manage to put up with that well enough" (NEB). Do you see why?

   (2) But *him* is italicized, indicating that it is not in the original. The Greek has no object for the verb. As in First Cor. 4:12, the object of the verb *bear* or *endure* is left to be supplied from context. The KJV has a marginal note indicating, as an alternative, that the object to be supplied is *me* rather than *him*.[6]

---

[6] Most scholarly opinion favors the first view. By understanding the statement sarcastically, a contradiction with Galatians 1:6–9 is avoided, but this view creates problems in the context. For verse 5 supports verse 4 by supplying reason to endure or bear with. How can verse 5 supply a reason for verse 4 on the assumption of the first view? Most commentators read between the lines, somewhat as follows: "You bear well with him. Why not with me?" Then the thought follows on as in verse 5. But this connection is added by the commentators rather than being a natural development from what is actually said. We must avoid such "reading between the lines" if possible.

I am always reluctant to go against the consensus of scholarly opinion, but feel I must in this instance. The KJV margin has the right idea by understanding *me* rather than *him* as the supplied word. Paul is completing his plea to the Corinthians to bear with him (1). "If someone brings a different message, you would do well to heed my plea and bear with me as I put a little foolishness before you." Then verse 5 connects with 4 in the most natural way imaginable.

A scholarly defense of this position will be found in J. Gresham Machen's book *The Origin of Paul's Religion*, 131–135.

LESSON 11

3. *Additional Support for Paul's Plea to Bear With Him [i. e., hear him out] (5-6).*
   a. What further reason does Paul supply (in 5) for bearing with him?[7]
   b. How is additional support for that reason supplied by verse 6?[8]

---

[7] Paul reckons that he is not behind the very chiefest apostles, i. e. inferior to them, in any respect. See AG, 849a and GT, 646a on the Greek verb *hustereo*. The Greek for *very chiefest* (*huperlian*) seems to many a strange expression to apply to the other genuine apostles of Christ, though GT seems to have no trouble with it, defining the word "over much; preeminently," then explaining its use here as "the most eminent apostles" (GT, 641). AG, 841 defines the adverb: "exceedingly, beyond measure," and says it is here used as an adjective meaning "the super-apostles" (cf. NASB margin, NIV). Others: "those superlative apostles" (RSV, NEB); "these superfine apostles of yours" (Goodspeed). Thus the word is understood as used ironically, poking fun, and referring to the false teachers (cf. 13) rather than to the Twelve.

Two considerations overturn this view: (1) What would be the point of saying he was not inferior to false teachers who were not apostles at all? How would that strengthen Paul's position at all? (2) The objection to applying this language to the Twelve is overturned by Gal. 2:2, 6 & 9, in which Paul spoke of the Twelve in similar fashion because of the claims of opponents. In neither case are the Twelve disrespected or degraded.

[8] The Greek for *rude in speech* (ASV, KJV) means untrained, uneducated, unversed or unskilled in the speaker's art. I will not take space for the interesting history of *idiotes*, but some may want to consult AG, 370; GT, 297; Trench's *Synonyms*, lxxix; TDNT, III, 215-17; EDNT, II, 172; VED, "Ignorant," A.4.

Paul is not necessarily admitting that he is an unskilled speaker. Certainly we who study his letters and sermons would not agree with that assessment. Verse 6 may be a response to criticism of his speaking style. Likely this part of the verse should be treated as a concession: "But even if untrained with respect to speech, not with respect to knowledge, ..." Even if it were true that he was untrained in speaking style, he was not unlearned when it came to knowledge, as he had made fully evident to the Corinthians. Criticism of his speaking dealt in superficialities—a matter of elevating style over substance.   Verse 6 finishes off his claim (in 5) not to be inferior to the other apostles. When it came to knowledge, the substance

Note continued on next page

Answer to Another Criticism (7-15)[9]
1. What other criticism was made against Paul? (7).

> of the gospel, Paul had fully demonstrated to the Corinthians that he was in every way equal to the other apostles.
>
> At this point it may be worthwhile to transcribe some of Machen's insightful analysis for those who do not have access to the book referred to above. On the ground of verses 5 & 6 Machen considers it likely that some type of Judazers were contending that Paul had not taught the whole truth; that the Judaizers had "fuller information about Jesus, about the Spirit, and about the gospel." If one comes claiming to have some additional teaching, Paul says, "You do well to bear with *me*" (4), as he had asked them to do in verse 1, rather than being led astray after "another Jesus." The reason is: "I do not fall behind the other apostles in any respect" (5). Even should I concede that I am an unpolished speaker, I have demonstrated full knowledge of the truth to you Corinthians (6).
>
> Machen sees the difficulties with the connection of thought when *him* is supplied in verse 4 rather than *me*. The interpretation that results when *him* is supplied "is unsatisfactory. It is obliged to supply a link to connect verse 4 with verse 5—namely, the thought, 'Bear with me.' That thought is here entirely unexpressed; ... If, however, the pronoun 'me,' not 'him,' is supplied with the verb at the end of verse 4, all is plain. Since the pronoun does not appear at all in the Greek, the translator is free to supply it as the context demands; and the context apparently demands the pronoun 'me'" (*Origin of Paul's Religion*, 133).
>
> "The connection with verse 5 really fixes the pronoun which is to be supplied at the end of the preceding verse. Paul is defending himself against the charge, implied in verse 6, that he had not made the full truth known. The opponents had claimed to have further information about Jesus, the Spirit, and the gospel. 'But,' says Paul, if that is their claim, ye do well to listen to my defense. For I have made Jesus and the Spirit and the gospel just as fully known to you as they have.' The thought is perfectly clear if only the pronoun 'me' be supplied at the end of verse 4" (*Ibid.*, 134).
>
> I think I only disagree with Machen's analysis when he applies *apostles* (5) to the false apostles (13). These men were not teaching the same thing Paul taught. They were dangerous men who would have taken the Corinthians away from Christ (vv. 2-3, 13-15)—not just away from Paul.
>
> [9] That Paul continues as he does in verse 7 confirms the view taken on verse 6 that his reference to being "rude in speech" stems from criticism against him. Two
>
> *Note continued on next page*

LESSON 11

2a. What was one source of support when Paul was in Corinth? (8–9).[10]

2b. What, according to Acts 18:2–3, was another source of support?

3a. What was his determination with regard to this practice in future? (10).

3b. Paul speaks of his claim with regard to preaching without support as a matter of "glorying" or "boasting" (10). It was a claim he needed to be able to make "in the regions of Achaia." Consider: Was this "glorying" inconsistent with the rule laid down in 10:17? (cf. 1 Cor. 9:12).

4. With regard to motive, Paul wanted to clear up one point (11). What does he deny about his refusal of Corinthian support?[11]

5. What was the real reason for Paul's stand about support? (12).[12]

---

points indicate that this section (7–15) is an answer to criticism. First, the way he asks the question in verse 7: "Did I commit a sin?"— ironically spoken (cf. 12:13). Second, that he must defend his motives (vv. 11f). Amazing! If Paul took support out in virgin territory where he was first planting churches, he would lay himself open to criticism (cf. 1 Thess. 2:5; 3 John 7). But now we see that his critics in Corinth were trying to turn his refusal of support against him, as if that somehow indicated a bad attitude toward the church (11). Nothing that these men could use against Paul was beneath them. He would be condemned whether he was or was not supported.

[10] *Brethren* who *came from Macedonia*: Possibly connected with Acts 18:5.

[11] This verse seems to point to another of his critics' efforts to discredit him.

[12] To cut off the occasion of those wishing an occasion to be found as our equals. The second purpose clause *that wherein they glory, etc.* is more easily explained not as Paul's purpose, but as the purpose of those desiring an occasion. Thus: "... in order to undermine the claim of those who would like to claim that in their boasted mission they work on the same terms as we do" (RSV); "... who desire an opportunity to be regarded just as we are in the matter about which they are boasting" (NASB; NKJV).

These men apparently took support from churches, and tried to discredit Paul for not doing so. They made great claims about being "apostles of Christ" in some sense (13–15). But Paul was determined not to give these men any occasion to put themselves in the class with himself and his associates. Paul's comparison of himself to them (in 16–33) will indicate how little claim they had to being in the same league with him.

6. Verse 13 provides further explanation of Paul's purpose (in 12). What was Paul's reason for cutting the ground from under these men so that they could never "be found as we"?[13]
7. "And no marvel," says Paul (14). "No wonder" (NKJV, RSV, NIV, NASB). Why is the method of such teachers "no marvel"? (14b–15a).[14]
8. What will determine the end of these teachers? (15b).[15]

Glorying in Weakness (11:16–33)

Resumption of Appeal (16–21a)

After the explanation of the reason for glorying (1–15), the appeal of verse 1 is resumed. When Paul now begins again, and this time goes on through with it, he does so only with the greatest reluctance. He is not a fool, yet feels he is being forced to play the part of a fool.

1a. In verse 16 Paul returns to what he has called "a little foolishness" (1). What now is said that explains what he meant by "foolishness"? (16–18).[16]

---

[13] Grk *metaschematizo* (fashioning themselves): "change the form of, transform, change," here in the middle form: "change or disguise oneself ... who disguise themselves as apostles" (AG, 513); "middle followed by *eis tina*, to transform one's self into some one, to assume one's appearance" (GT, 406). These men are false apostles, not the real thing; they wear a mask and pretend. They are false apostles who can never "be found as we" (13). Paul wanted to cut off any occasion for them to claim as much.

[14] They are only imitating the methods of their master.

[15] Their end will not be according to their outward profession, but "according to their works" (15b).

[16] Although he is forced to boast as fools do, Paul has serious purpose (and certainly not selfish motive) behind this boasting. He hopes the Corinthians will understand the reason for it and not think him foolish (16a). But perhaps they will take him for a fool. Even in that case, it is necessary, and he begs the indulgence they would grant a fool (cf. 19).

LESSON 11

1b. How does he describe the model (norm or standard) according to which he will now speak? (17).[17]

2a. How does Paul explain (in 18) what has led him to glory (or boast)?[18]

2b. How does Proverbs 26:5 cast light upon what he is doing?

3a. What reason does Paul give for using this method of speaking? (19).[19]

3b. He elaborates (in 20). To what extent had the Corinthians shown a capacity for bearing foolishness?

3c. What is indicated (in 20) with regard to the character and methods of the false teachers?[20]

---

[17] *I speak not after the Lord.* The Lord will not be the standard according to which he speaks. He will not speak as the Lord spoke, nor as the Lord would have one speak. (Contrast 10:1.) Take note of the contrast to speaking "after the Lord": *but as in foolishness.* Not *in* foolishness, for he speaks with serious purpose, but *as* (Grk *hos*) in foolishness—i. e., playing the part of a fool; answering "a fool according to his folly" (Prov. 26:5); his opponents according to their own methods. See below (18).

[18] *Seeing that many glory after the flesh*, i. e. in accord with selfish human nature; in the way that is common among men. Contrast with speaking "after the Lord."

[19] The Corinthians' tolerance for foolishness (19). *For you bear with the foolish gladly, being wise* yourselves. As a wise man is patient with a senile or retarded person. Spoken with irony, this explanation is connected with Paul's expressed determination to go on with his glorying: "I will glory also" (18). Paul certainly need have no fear of being rejected by the Corinthians for playing the fool. They had quite a lot of experience at showing tolerance for fools. See what follows in verse 20.

[20] Verse 20 shows just how far the Corinthians had gone in bearing with fools. They had put up with the most outrageous overbearing behavior on the part of Paul's opponents. The character and methods of the false teachers is revealed here. They had made themselves lords and the Corinthians their slaves. Certainly these "wise" Corinthians had shown a lot of tolerance for folly, and should have no trouble at all bearing with Paul's "foolishness."

Lenski observed in the first half of the twentieth century: "What Paul pictures here has been endlessly repeated. People will swallow anything on the part of false teachers. These men get their followers just where they want them; they love to put

Note continued on next page

4. What did Paul and his associates appear to be (21a) by contrast with his opponents (20)?[21]

> on lordly airs; they still get the huge salaries; they still act abusively. The only change that we note is a little modern veneer."
>
> *If he brings you into bondage*, i. e., reduces you to slavery (Grk *katadouleuo*, AG, 410b; GT, 331a); perhaps with Moffatt: "assumes control of your souls"; or as Galatians 2:4, 4:8f & 5:1, with reference to the law.
>
> *If he devours you* or "eats you up." Grk *katesthio* in Mark 12:40 & Luke 20:47 of those who "eat up widows' houses i. e. appropriate them illegally" (AG) or "forcibly appropriate" (GT). Here: "to strip one of his goods" (GT, 339b); "i. e. exploits, robs (you)" (AG, 422a). *If he takes you* captive. Grk *lambano* has varied applications. For this verse cf. 12:16 where it is used of taking or catching one by means of a trick; in Luke 5:5 of taking fish in a net. Perhaps here: "if someone 'takes you in', takes advantage of you" (AG, 464b), or: "to circumvent one by fraud" (GT, 370b). Similar to *katadouleuo* above, but with different imagery—that of a fisherman catching a fish or a hunter capturing his prey, thus bringing it under his power.
>
> *If he exalts himself*, i. e. "to a position of authority to which they held no title and from which they sought, like earthly potentates, to lord it over the Corinthian flock (cf. Mk. 10:42ff.; 1 Pet. 5:3)" (Hughes); even "fashioning themselves into apostles of Christ" (v. 13). But the lexicons explain the metaphorical usage of the Grk *epairo*: "to be lifted up with pride, to exalt one's self" (GT, 228a); "be presumptuous, put on airs" (AG, 282a). So contrary to the teaching of the Master! (Matt. 23:12). Yet the Corinthians had put up with it. What a capacity for "tolerance"!
>
> *If he smites you on the face*—"an extraordinary, very disgraceful and insolent maltreatment" (Meyer). Perhaps the literal meaning is not out of the question in view of Acts 23:2 (cf. 1 Kings 22:24).
>
> [21] The following is a pretty literal rendering of 21a: *According to shame* (or *disgrace*), *I confess* (literally, *say*): *We* (emphatic in the Greek) *have been weak!* (See RSV; NKJ; NASB; NIV.) Grk *atimia* is "dishonor, disgrace, shame," the clause here being rendered: "to my shame I must confess" (AG, 120a; cf. GT, 83a). After the description of the abuse the Corinthians had put up with from his opponents (20), Paul says he would have to confess, to his shame: *We have been weak!*, meaning in comparison with the outrageous behavior of his opponents. Of course Paul is speaking sarcastically. But now we can better appreciate the slander against Paul from these men: "His bodily presence is weak" (10:1, 10). Now we see what they thought it meant to be a servant of Christ. Clearly, these men knew nothing of the Jesus Paul preached (11:4).

LESSON 11

Paul's Glorying (21b–33)

After all that has preceded (16–21a), and "weak" as he appears in comparison with his opponents (21a), Paul is, however, finally ready to set forth his boast. Whatever his opponents wanted to claim for themselves as Jews Paul could match (21b–22). They had no point in these claims that should commend them to the church as over against Paul. None of this stuff was to the point. The relevant point was service to Christ. What could they claim in this regard? When it came to the real issue, their claim to be ministers of Christ (23a; cf. 13–15), Paul left them far behind. But consider the nature of the boast Paul makes: "the things that concern my weakness" (30), which turns out, finally, to be a glorying in Christ Jesus (12:8–10; cf. Gal. 6:11–14, 17).

1a. Paul could be bold too! But as he prepares to give expression to this boldness, how does he feel about it? (21b).

1b. What is the first ground of his comparison of himself with his opponents? (22).[22]

1c. How does he compare with them in that regard?

2a. What is the new basis for comparison introduced in verse 23?

2b. Again, as he begins to compare himself with his opponents, how does he feel about what he is doing? (23).[23]

2c. Yet how does he compare with them? (23).[24]

3. The details of Paul's boast fall into two classes, beginning with what he calls (in 28, which see) the exceptional, "extra matters" (23b–27).

---

[22] Paul compares himself with his opponents first as Jews (22) and then as ministers of Christ (23). In one area he matches them; in the other he exceeds them.

[23] Grk *paraphroneo*: "to be beside one's self, out of one's senses, void of understanding, insane" (GT, 486b); "be beside oneself, conduct one's self in an irrational manner" (AG, 623b).

[24] In comparing himself with them as Jews, no matter what term they may use, Paul kept saying: *I also* (Grk *kago*). But when it comes to their claim to be ministers of Christ, he says: *I over* or *above* (Grk prep. *huper* with the accusative) them (implied). In this regard he leaves them far behind. But it is not that anyone could be more than a minister of Christ. Paul is thinking of the actual service implied in the term, and in this regard he stands far above them, as the following elaboration shows.

I would discourage taking a lot of class time for the details, but some commentary is provided in a note below.[25] As for questions on these matters, consider:

- a. What is the nature of the things of which Paul boasts in 23b–27 in contrast with those listed in 28–29?
- b. Think about it! This is Paul's boast! Does it seem strange that he would treat such things as reason to boast?
- c. What about his opponents? Would they have gloried in such things?

4. *The Regular, Daily Burden (28–29).* Paul calls the hard things previously listed "the exceptional (or extra) things."[26] Now he turns to the continual, daily burden.

---

[25] A general statement (23b) is followed by specifics: *Five beatings from the Jews*, who stopped at 39 stripes to make sure they did not exceed the limit prescribed by law (24; cf. Deut. 25:3), "a most ignominious punishment for a free man" (Josephus, *Antiquities*, Bk 4, Ch. 8, Pgh 21). *Three times beaten with rods* (25), the Roman version, of which only one instance is recorded by Luke (Acts 16:22f). *Once stoned* (25) ... in Lystra (Acts 14:19). The Jewish method of executing the death penalty (Lev. 24:16; Num. 15:35f; Deut. 21:21; John 8:59; 10:31-33; Acts 8:58f; 14:5). *Three times I suffered shipwreck (25).* None of which are otherwise known. Acts 27 is later. *A night and a day have I been in the deep*, the aftermath of shipwreck; i. e. "on the high sea, on a raft or clinging to wreckage" (Lenski). *Many dangers encountered in travel* (26). *Perils of rivers* (26), which had to be crossed in the course of his many journeys. *Perils among false brethren* (26) such as were causing the trouble at Corinth. *Other hardships encountered in his ministry (27). Watchings often,* doing without sleep "in order to make a livelihood from his trade, after days spent in apostolic ministry, or in order to reach distant stopping-places, or to conquer heaven by his prayers" (Allo, quoted in Hughes, 413). *Cold and nakedness*, i. e., without adequate clothing.

[26] Grk *choris* means "without, apart from," "besides" (AG, 890f; cf. GT, 675). So: *apart from the parektos*, meaning *besides*—the word used for "saving" in Matthew 5:32, "saving for the cause of fornication." Hence: "the exceptional things." Literally

Note continued on next page

LESSON 11

a. What was the daily burden that Paul continually bore?[27]

> the clause reads: "apart from the besides things." *Grimm* explains: "the things that occur besides or in addition." *Thayer* compares our word "extra" as in "extra matters." Hence: the things that are just "incidental," or "extra," or thrown in "besides"—not Paul's main burden.
>
> So the point is, the suffering and hardships Paul has already presented are just incidental, thrown in besides; not his main burden. "All the items mentioned from verse 24 onwards are *ta parektos*, the things that come in only 'besides.' They are not at all Paul's chief burden, they are only the extras that are thrown in for good measure. ... This phrase is astounding. We think that Paul has been heaping up all of his very worst troubles, during some of which he was even nearly killed. With the turn of a little phrase he now tells us that these are only the little extras, the greens that garnish the roast, the perquisites that are handed him in addition to his full salary" (Lenski).
>
> After these things that come *often* (26f), now he is ready to add the continual *daily* burden (28f).
>
> [27] *That which presses upon me daily*. GT, 243, defines *epistasis*: "an advancing, approach; incursion, onset, press," and says it is here "used of the pressure of a multitude asking help, counsel, etc.," but points out that "others would have us translate it here by *oversight, attention, care*, a common meaning of the word in Polybius." VED (under "press") takes it of "the pressure of onset due to the constant call upon the Apostle for all kinds of help, advice counsel, exhortation, decisions as to difficulties, disputes, etc." AG, 300a, considers *pressure* "an outstanding possibility: *the daily pressure on me*. Other possibilities: *the attention* or *care daily required of me* ...; *superintendence, oversight ... the burden of oversight, which lies upon me day in and day out*; finally, *epistasis* can also mean *stopping, hindrance, delay* ...; then: *the hindrances that beset me day by day*." A much fuller discussion of the possibilities than can be presented within the limitations of the lexicons will be found in Hughes, 415, n. 79. Probably some such general word as *pressure* should be chosen to explain the Greek. Then the following clause is added by way of apposition and further definition: "anxiety for all the churches." Altogether, then, the specifics found in GT and VED would seem to be reasonable applications of the idea. Finally, take note of the emphasis on *daily*, as opposed to the other category described in the previous clause.
>
> *Note continued on next page*

    b. How is this great burden illustrated in verse 29?[28]
5. How is the subject of Paul's glorying defined in verse 30?[29]
6. Give thought to why Paul appeals to God as his witness (in 31).[30]

Anxiety for all the churches. Grk *merimna* means *care* in the sense of *anxiety*—"the anxiety which torments him." Paul is not thinking of "jurisdiction"—the care of the churches in that sense. "But every Christian centre had claims on his thought and sympathy, those most of all of which he had intimate knowledge. The intercourse between the chief centres was fairly constant, he was frequently receiving information which gave him plenty to think about (1 Cor. 1:11, 16: 17), and anxiety about people generates care for them, when care is possible" (Plummer). For the lexicons on this word see GT, 400a & AG, 504b. What Paul has in mind is illustrated by the following verse.

[28] *Weak* can be explained from previous references (1 Cor. 8:7, 9, 11, 12; 9:22). *And I am not weak.* He feels himself, due to his sympathy with the weak, "transplanted into the same position" (Meyer). Grk *puroo* (burn) figuratively "burn, be inflamed" (AG, 731); according to context, with anger (2 Macc. 4:38; 10:35; 14:45), with sexual desire (1 Cor. 7:9). What emotion is indicated here? Some say *indignation*, i. e. at those who caused the fall; or *shame*, as though he were the fallen one (Hughes); but Meyer thinks, as the climax to *and I am not weak*, what is required is feeling the pain of the fallen one. See also GT, 558b.

[29] Since it has become necessary to glory, Paul says, *I will glory of the things that concern my weakness.* That is what he has been doing. He boasts of things concerning which men like his opponents in Corinth would take no pride, of which they certainly would not boast. They would boast of their strengths, their intellect, their ability. But Paul was such a different man than they. When the subject has been brought to a conclusion (in 12:8–10) we see why Paul chooses to boast about his weakness. He is really glorying in the Lord, whose power is put on display in the work he accomplishes through such a weak man.

[30] Is it due to the greatness of the suffering enumerated; out of a sense that it would be perceived as exaggerated? (Hodge). Or because the whole idea of glorying about one's weakness seems ludicrous? Is Paul being facetious? Just "putting us on"? "Strange as it may sound, his boast is nothing but his excessive weakness. God knows it is the truth" (Lenski).

7. The escape from Damascus at the end of the list, actually took place at the beginning of Paul's life as a Christian (Acts 9:23–25). How is this incident related to Paul's boast with regard to "the things that concern (his) weakness"?[31]

---

[31] Imagine the humiliation! The proud persecutor, heading for Damascus intent on snuffing out the Christians, but now hiding out, escaping in such a fashion!

But what is the connection here? Why does this incident from the beginning of Paul's ministry appear at the end of the discussion? Many see verse 30 as the beginning of the next development rather than as a concluding summary. Meyer, for example, thinks Paul intended to begin at the beginning of his ministry and go on with a historical presentation of the weakness that had manifested itself through his ministry, but gets distracted and never carries out his original plan. Hughes agrees that verse 30 is the beginning of a section, but then sees Paul's intention being developed with references to the escape from Damascus and then his thorn in the flesh as examples of his weakness, with a climax being reached at 12:8–10.

The incident occurred early in his career, before any of his great successes. From the outset he was to learn a great lesson—namely, "that his mightiest asset was utter weakness, weakness which enabled God to do everything with him and through him" (Lenski).

This beginning is then followed by 12:1–10, in which the main point, consistent with the beginning assertion (11:30), is not Paul's great visions and revelations, but his thorn in the flesh, which simply reinforced the lesson learned at the beginning. Fourteen years ago (12:2) would also be early in Paul's ministry. Early on the great lesson was to be impressed upon Paul's mind.

LESSON 12
Second Corinthians 12:1–13

PAUL'S GLORYING (11:1–12:13) continued

Paul's "Thorn in the Flesh" and its Significance: The Sufficiency of Divine Grace (12:1–10)

As pointed out in a footnote, Second Cor. 11:30 seems to be the beginning of a subsection, in which Paul, after the appeal to God as witness (in 31), cites two incidents in which, early in his ministry, he learned the lesson about the power in human weakness. In addition to the humiliating escape from Damascus (11:32–33), a second incident, also from early in Paul's ministry, fourteen years before this letter, is added as also teaching the same lesson (12:1–10).

The heading indicates the main point of this passage, i. e. not the vision, but the thorn in the flesh given to Paul "by reason of the exceeding greatness of the revelations." Paul mentions the tremendous revelation that had been given him, but separates himself from it personally, and mentions it only to decline to glory of such matters. So actually such revelations are only mentioned as the occasion for his humiliating "thorn in the flesh."

Introduction to the Subject (1)

1. What is Paul's attitude as he turns to a new phase of his subject? (1a).[1]
2. What is the new subject to which he comes? (1b).[2]

---

[1] The glorying was necessary because of the attacks of his opponents and the failure of the Corinthians to stand up for him (12:11). *It is not expedient*, says Paul, i. e., advantageous, beneficial or profitable; but it was necessary to the teaching that was beneficial. Since it is not expedient, the "visions and revelations" are introduced only to give his glorying a turn that will be profitable (5).

[2] Apparently another phase of Paul's answer to his opponents (cf. 11: 18, 22, 23). Did they claim "visions and revelations"? Did they question his? For visions of Paul, consult Acts 22:17–21; 18:9f; 23:11; 27:23f; cf. 9:12; 16:9f.

LESSON 12

An Example of "Visions and Revelations" (2–4)

1. What example of "visions and revelations" is singled out by Paul?

2a. Paul speaks of "a man in Christ" and does not directly identify him. But what evidence in the context indicates that Paul is talking about himself?[3]

2b. Why would Paul present the matter as he does, speaking of himself in the third person instead of simply saying "I"?[4]

3. How is "the third heaven" (2) further defined in the context (4)?[5]

4. How are "unspeakable words" further defined? (4).[6]

Paul's Attitude With Regard to Such Claims (5–6)

1. How would you explain Paul's attitude regarding such claims? (5).[7]

---

[3] Verses 5–7 are not understandable otherwise. By presenting the matter impersonally Paul claims the experience but without resting anything on it (6b).

[4] Evidently in order not to make such "visions and revelations" a matter of glorying on his own behalf. Paul hints that he is talking about himself, but he will not say so plainly. The incident is not to be a subject of boasting.

[5] *Paradise* is where the tree of life is found (Rev. 2:7; cf. 22:2). Only elsewhere at Luke 23:43 in the NT, the word is used for the "garden of Eden" in the Septuagint (Gen. 2–3). See *paradeisos* in AG, 614 & esp. GT, 480.

[6] *Unspeakable*, i. e., not impossible to utter, but unlawful to utter.

[7] Paul views the matter almost as if there were two of himself. He was so carried away under the influence of outside forces as if he were out of himself. It was happening to him. Yet he watches it, as though seeing himself in a dream. Telling of so great a revelation suggests reason for glorying. Yet he separates himself from the experience. He will not make it a subject of glorying. In fact, it was not due to merit, but was a gift of divine grace.

Lenski suggests a plausible reason for the experience. This man would have to endure so much (11:23–33). "As if to forearm him against all of it so that he might not break down in his spirit under this frightful, neverending load, the Lord let him have a taste of Paradise." Similarly Calvin (in Hughes, 439).

Yet apparently Paul had gone fourteen years without telling the experience, and does so now only for extraordinary reasons.

2a. Paul says he would only be speaking the truth if he boasted of such an experience. Why, then, did he forbear boasting? (6).

2b. Related to that, on what did Paul want their view of him to be based?[8]

2c. How does this compare with the approach of modern "Holy Ghost baptized" men with regard to their experiences and testimonies?

"A Thorn in the Flesh" (7–9a)[9]

1. Paul's "thorn in the flesh" cannot be certainly explained.[10] But what was the purpose of it as related to "the exceeding greatness of the revelations"? (7).[11]

---

[8] Their judgment of him was not to be grounded on unsupported claims, but on their experience of him. Their estimate of Paul was to be based entirely upon what was seen in him or heard from him, evidence that could be objectively tested, not on mere claims which could not be tested.

[9] Grk *skolops*: "*a* (pointed) *stake*, then *thorn, splinter*, etc., specifically of an injurious foreign body" (AG, 756b); "*a pointed piece of wood, a pale, a stake: edothe moi skolops te sarki, a sharp stake* (others say *splinter*, A. V. *thorn*; cf. Num. 33:55; Ezek. 28:24; Hos. 2:6; ...) *to pierce my flesh*, appears to indicate some constant bodily ailment or infirmity, which, even when Paul had been caught up in a trance to the third heaven, sternly admonished him that he still dwelt in a frail and mortal body, 2 Cor. 12:7 (cf. 1–4)" (GT, 579a).

"The proper meaning is 'stake', or a sharpened wooden shaft. In Hellenistic Greek, however, the modified meaning of thorn or splinter is found (cf. the Septuagint version of Num. 33:55, Ezek. 28:24, Hos. 2:6, and Ecclus. 43:19, and also the evidence in Moulton and Milligan and in Arndt and Gingrich), though not to the exclusion of the original meaning" (Hughes, 447). (See Hughes, 442–448, for a long treatment of the subject, with much wisdom. Worthwhile!)

Literally, a thorn *for* or perhaps *with respect to* the flesh. See Meyer and Hughes for the implications. Of other possible references cf. esp. Gal. 4:13f.

[10] "Quacks" is Lenski's word for the theologians who try to diagnose this thorn.

[11] Observe: Paul's own determination (5–6) was consistent with the divine purpose. This thorn had done its work in him. Verse 7 is an example of overruling providence, a messenger of Satan being used for divine purpose.

2. What was Paul's initial attitude toward the thorn in the flesh? (8).[12]

3. What, finally, was the Lord's response to Paul's petition? (9a).[13]

Consequent Change of View Following from the Reassurance with Regard to the Sufficiency of Divine Grace (9b–10)

1. Describe the drastic change that took place in Paul after receiving this word from the Lord (contrast 8 with 9b).[14]

---

[12] *Thrice* he besought the Lord, like the Lord himself in Gethsemane (Matt. 26:44). He no doubt thought the "thorn" was a hindrance to his ministry. "If only I did not have this handicap," he thought, "how much better I could do." So at first he persisted in beseeching the Lord for its removal. Incidentally, this verse is an example of prayer addressed to the Lord Christ (for see verse 9).

[13] *And he has said to me.* Greek "perfect tense, the significance of which is that the force of something done in the past continues in the present: thus the word spoken to Paul after his third petition abides with present power." Contrast the aorist tense in *I besought*: "Paul did beseech in the past, but he does so no more, for he has received an answer of permanent validity" (Hughes, 451).

My grace is sufficient for thee: Greek *arkeo*: "be enough, sufficient, adequate," the statement being equal to saying: "You need nothing more than my grace" (AG, 107a). GT, 73b, thinks the meaning is: "sufficient to enable thee to bear the evil manfully; there is, therefore, no reason why thou shouldst ask for its removal." Perhaps better: sufficient for your task; sufficient to do what you have to do. You do not need a perfect body, or any of the things human beings often fancy to be necessary to success. The grace of Christ is enough. Then notice the further explanation.

For my power is made perfect in weakness. Grk *teleo*: "bring to an end, finish, complete"—i. e., "*power finds its consummation* or *reaches perfection in* (the presence of) *weakness*" (AG, 810f). "Power is brought to its end or goal (*telos*) in weakness." "This is the summit of the epistle, the lofty peak from which the whole is viewed in true proportion. From this vantagepoint the entire range of Paul's apostleship is seen in focus. ... The greater the servant's weakness, the more conspicuous is the power of his Master's all-sufficient grace" (Hodge).

[14] *Most gladly therefore will I rather glory in my weaknesses* (9b), i. e. rather than plead for their removal (8) ... much more than simple resignation.

2. What is the aim or purpose of glorying in weaknesses? (9b).[15]
3. What even stronger expression of Paul's change of view occurs in 10a?[16]
4. What reason is given for this remarkable view of weaknesses for the sake of Christ? (10b).[17]

Final Word on Glorying: Paul's Apostolic Credentials (12:11–13)

Paul Forced into Foolish Glorying (11a; cf. 1a)

1. What had forced Paul into this foolish glorying? Or to put the question in another way: How had the Corinthians failed him?
2. What should they have done when false teachers attacked Paul?

Reason to Commend Paul (11b–13)

1. "I ought to have been commended of you," said Paul. What reason did they have for commending him? (11b; cf. 11:5).
2. What apostolic credentials had he offered? (12).
3. What challenge does he put upon the Corinthians (in 13)?[18]
4. Verse 13 ends with more of Paul's irony. He could think of only one way in which he had "wronged" the Corinthians (cf. 11:7). For what "wrong" does he ironically beg forgiveness?

---

[15] *That the power of Christ may rest upon me.* More literally: cover me like a tent, or pitch its tent over me (Grk *episkenoo*, GT, 242; AG, 298). See Hughes, 452, including note 141.

[16] The terms after *weaknesses* elaborate with particular manifestations of weakness. The man who is forced to submit to injuries, necessities, etc. is certainly a weak man—not at all like the powerful man of the world.

[17] *Then am I strong*—i. e., with the strength of Christ. "Human weakness provides the opportunity for divine power" (Hughes).

[18] Does verse 13 (with 1 Cor. 1:4–7) imply that "the signs of an apostle" were not just the miracles done by him, but included the gifts communicated to others as well (cf. Acts 8:14–19; 19:1–6; 2 Tim. 1:6)? Consider the implications.

LESSON 13
Second Corinthians 12:14–13:14

THE COMING OF PAUL
SECOND COR. 12:14–13:14

The last section of Part Three deals with the anticipated third trip to Corinth. It reveals clearly what Paul was trying to accomplish by means of this letter. It defines the relation between the letter and the planned trip to Corinth.

Paul's Relations with the Corinthians (12:14–18)

1. Some think Paul refers (in 14a) to a third time he was ready to come, though he had actually come only once. Does that agree with 13:1a (cf. 2:1)?[1]

2. *Paul not to be a burden to them any more than in the past (14b–15).* Of what does Paul assure the Corinthians (in 14b)?[2]

   a. What is meant by "a burden," according to the context? (14c–15).

   b. What two explanations are added in support of this assurance? (14cd).[3]

   c. Why is the parent/child illustration (14d) especially appropriate? (cf. 1 Cor. 4:15).

   d. What attitude does Paul express with regard to sacrifice and service for the Corinthians? (15a).

   e. What strange possibility does Paul mention in 15b?[4]

---

[1] The second visit (cf. 2:1) almost certainly took place during Paul's Ephesian ministry (Acts 19).

[2] He would no more be a burden to them than he had been before (14b–15; cf. 11:7–9 & 12:13).

[3] With regard to the first, Paul's desire was not to get something from them, but to win them for Christ.

[4] A strange case indeed, but it occurs. The more one loves and sacrifices for a person, the less it is appreciated. Do the Corinthians want to be like that?

3. *Another possibility considered, no doubt one proposed by Paul's opponents: Paul just laying a trap, setting them up for later profit (16–18).*[5]

   a. "True," Paul's opponents seemed to reason, "Paul himself did not take advantage of you. But he was only laying a trap, setting you up for later profit" (16).[6] In what way, according to the following context? (17–18).

   b. What is Paul's answer to such an insinuation? (17–18).[7]

Clarification of Purpose (12:19-21)

1. Verse 19a should probably be understood as a question (KJV, RSV, ASV & NASB margin). Paul corrects two false impressions with regard to this letter. First, his defense of himself might give the impression that he had set the readers up as judges over him or felt himself accountable to them. Second, they might also get the impression that his self-defense was due to self-interest.

---

[5] We see how Paul's opponents had tried to poison the minds of the Corinthians. True, he had not personally taken support from them (16a), but it was all a trap (16b). He was setting them up to take advantage of them through his representatives (17). But the Corinthians knew such insinuations were unfounded. True, Paul was behind Titus' mission (18a; cf. ch. 7). But the Corinthians knew Titus had no more taken advantage of them than Paul had (18bcd).

[6] Interesting language in 16: Grk adjective *panourgos* (crafty), "quite predominantly, and in our literature exclusively, in an unfavorable connotation *clever, crafty, sly* literally 'ready to do anything'. Paul says, taking up an expression used by his opponents, *huparchon panourgos crafty fellow that I am* 2 Cor 12: 16" (AG, 608a; cf. GT, 476a). Only here in NT, but the noun *panourgia* occurs in Luke 20:23, 1 Cor. 3:19, 2 Cor. 4:2, 11:3 & Eph. 4:14. *I caught you*, as an animal or fish is taken (Grk *lambano* as in 11:20) by means of some trickery. Grk *dolos* (guile, deceit or the like) in the dative case: by means of cunning, deceit or treachery (AG, 203); "properly *bait*, Homer, Od. 12, 252; *a lure, snare*; hence *craft, deceit, guile*." (GT, 155a). Cf. *dolios* in 11:13 and *doloo* in 4:2.

[7] An important lesson on wise and irreproachable conduct in ministers of the gospel. Had Paul and his associates not conducted themselves in a manner that would be beyond reproach, he would not have been able to ask these questions!

LESSON 13

    a. How does he answer the first? (19b).[8]

    b. What about the second? (19c).[9]

2. Verses 20 & 21 provide the reason Paul writes with the purpose indicated in 19c. He was afraid he would come and not find them the way he wanted to find them. How is that idea then further explained?[10]

Action to be Taken at Paul's Coming (13:1–4)

Paul means to set in motion a judicial hearing (1b) according to the words of the law in Deuteronomy 19:15. There would be no further sparing. The guilty would be dealt with according to rigorous legal procedure.

1a. *Unsparing legal procedure to be instigated (1–2).* How is this idea brought out in 1b?

1b. What advance warning had been given repeatedly? (2; cf. 1 Cor. 4:21).

2. *The reason Paul would be unsparing against any who were found in sin: The challenge to his authority (3).*

    a. What is the connection of verse 3 with what precedes?[11]

    b. Explain this challenge in light of 10:10, consulting also First Cor. 4:18–21.[12]

---

[8] *In the sight of God*, i. e. before him as the judge to whom he is accountable. *In Christ*, i. e. as a Christian.

[9] *For your edifying*, i. e., to strengthen them so they would not be taken in by false teachers—his real purpose, which is further explained in 20–21.

[10] The other side of the picture is that they would find him other than they wanted him to be. As his finding them other than he wished is explained in 20b–21, their finding him to be other than they wished seems to be explained by what follows in Chapter 13.

[11] The Greek connective *epei* is here "causal *because, since, for*" as in 11:18 (AG, 284a); "used of cause, etc., *since, seeing that, because*" (GT, 229b). Verse 3a gives the reason Paul would be unsparing against any who were found in sin.

[12] Grk *zeteo* (you seek) here in the sense: require or demand (GT, 272); ask for, request, demand (AG, 338f); similarly in Mark 8:11f; Luke 11:16; 12:48; John 4:23;

Note continued on next page

3. *Explanation of Paul's "Weakness": A Repetition of the Story of Christ (4).* "For" (Grk *gar*) introduces an explanation. How does Paul explain his behavior toward the Corinthians?[13]

The Real Point in Question Under the Circumstances (13:5–6)

1. *Self-examination demanded (5a).* The Corinthians were seeking "a proof of Christ that speaks in me; etc." (3). But when a church begins to challenge the authority and power of an apostle of Christ, what is really in question?[14]

---

1 Cor. 1:22; 4:2. Grk *dokime* (a proof) already in 2:9, 8:2 & 9:13. Take note of the play on words of the same family in verses 3–7. Lenski renders what they were seeking: "a proof of the Christ speaking in me." Paul's authority as an apostle of Christ had been challenged. His opponents had said "his letters are weighty and strong; but his bodily presence is weak" (10:10; cf. 1 Cor. 4:18–21). They had questioned whether all this power in his letters really amounted to anything. By such conduct they challenged a manifestation of the judicial power of Christ. "Well, all right," says Paul, "you shall see. You want a proof of Christ speaking in me. You shall have one." The unsparing judicial procedure to be followed when he arrived in Corinth would be a demonstration of whether there was anything to the strong words he writes. In effect a challenge of Paul was a challenge to the Christ whose spokesman and apostle he was.

[13] *Crucified through weakness* (4a) refers to the Lord's voluntary submission to the human condition (cf. 8:9; Phil. 2:5–9). He could have called for legions of angels (Matt. 26:53), but was willing to appear weak. Paul continues (in 4b) with a parallel between his conduct and that of Christ, as if to say: Do you want to understand the "weakness" observed in us, i. e. why we have not been strong to mete out punishment? Consider Christ (4a) and you will understand! Paul's treatment of the Corinthians was a repetition of the story of Christ. Cf. 10:1.

But we shall live with him through the power of God toward you. As he (4a), so we (4b). Paul speaks of the power he would manifest upon his arrival in Corinth. That the future tense refers to that rather than to the resurrection at the second coming of Christ is proved by the last phrase *toward you*.

[14] One's own relationship to Christ is in question when he challenges the apostles by whose testimony faith comes (1 Cor. 3:5; cf. John 17: 20). Not "a proof of

Note continued on next page

LESSON 13

2. *Alternative to such self-examination (5b).* What is the one reason one might fear such a test?[15]

3. *A second conclusion to be clarified by such testing (6).* When they do this self-testing, what did Paul hope they would also realize?[16]

Paul's Great Concern and Motivation (13:7–10)

1. *Prayer and purpose (7).* What is Paul's motivation as he prays that the Corinthians do no evil?[17]

Christ" speaking in the apostle (3a), but proof of their own relationship with Christ is required. That is the real point at issue when people start thinking as they were. Not the apostolic authority, but them. So today when God's word is criticized. Men think it is on trial, but it is their integrity that is in question.

Try your own selves, etc. Grk *peirazo*: "*try, make trial of, put to the test*, to discover what kind of a person someone is" (AG, 640a; cf. GT, 498).

whether you are in the faith. The point in question when one begins to challenge the apostles by whose testimony faith comes (1 Cor. 3:5; cf. John 17:20).

Prove your own selves. Grk *dokimazo*: "*to test, examine, prove, scrutinize* (to see whether a thing be genuine or not), as metals" (GT, 154b; cf. AG, 202b); money and the like. See the use of this verb in First Cor. 3: 13; First Peter 1:7; and in the Septuagint at Prov. 8:10; 17:3; Zech. 13:9. The whole passage turns on the significance of this and related words: *dokime* ("proof" in 3); *dokimazo* ("prove" in 5a); *adokimos* ("reprobate" in 5, 6 & 7); *dokimos* ("approved" in 7).

[15] Doubt about their relationship with Christ. One would not fear such a test if he knew Christ was in him. Grk *adokimos* (reprobate): "not standing the test, not approved" (GT, 12b; cf. AG, 13b). Do they fear being found disapproved?

[16] *But I hope that you shall know that we are not reprobate*—as should be obvious from the self-examination to which he challenges them. They sought "a proof of Christ" speaking in him (3a). Such a proof would be evident when they looked within themselves. For the criteria which showed them to be Christians and within the faith would reveal that the men who had brought them to faith in the first place were themselves Christians. Compare 10:7 for similar reasoning.

[17] *Not that we may appear approved.* Grk *phaino*: "*to bring forth into the light, cause to shine; to show*"; here passive: "*become clear* or *manifest*, with a predicate

Note continued on next page

2. *Explanation of "as reprobate" (8–9).* If Paul had no reason to show his "power" in Corinth, he would seem to fail the test (3) and be "as reprobate" (7). But he could do nothing about that. Why? (8).[18]

   a. What further explanation is added in 9a?[19]

   b. What additional prayer (cf. 7a) is offered for the Corinthians? (9b).[20]

3. Purpose of the epistle as related to these explanations (10). What is Paul's purpose?[21]

---

nominative (*be seen to be*)" (GT, 647; cf. AG, 851f). His purpose was not to put himself in a good light, i. e. *dokimos* (as in 10:18): "*approved* (by test), *tried and true, genuine*" (AG, 203a; cf. GT, 155a).

That which is honorable, or good, excellent, lovely, etc. (Grk *kalos*).

But we may be as reprobate. Grk *adokimos* as in 5 & 6. Not reprobate, but *as* (Grk *hos*) reprobate; i. e. appear as one disapproved, not standing the test. Paul is thinking of how he may appear when he comes to Corinth and has no occasion to demonstrate a powerful "proof of Christ" (3), thus appearing "weak" in "bodily presence" (cf. 10:10). He wanted the Corinthians to do the right thing, even though he would be left with no occasion to show his strength.

[18] The reason is based on the general attitude operative in all Paul's work: *For we have no power* (Grk *dunamai*: cf. *dunateo* in 3, *dunamis* twice in 4) *against the truth*—literal translation indicating the connection of verse 8 in the context. If Paul came to Corinth and found the disciples standing for the truth, he would have no occasion to meet the challenge (of 3) with a show of power. For he had no power to stand against the truth, even if some perceived him as "weak."

[19] *For we rejoice, when we are weak, etc. Weak* as having no occasion to demonstrate the show of force to which he was challenged (in 3). Draw upon context back to chapter 10, especially 10:10, to understand Paul's expressions.

And you are strong, having done the right thing, but giving him no occasion to be "strong" in bringing his powerful weapons (cf. 10:4) to bear against them.

[20] Grk *katartisis* is restoration to right order. Compare *katartizo* (11b) which is applied to mending nets (Matt. 4:21; Mark 1:19), setting bones and the like.

[21] The thought in mind at the beginning of the section (10:1–11, esp. 8–11).

LESSON 13

Closing Words (13:11–14)

The closing includes a series of exhortations (11–12),[22] communication of a salutation from the saints, evidently those whom Paul has told about the letter he planned to write (13), and a final wish for the Corinthians (14). After all has been said, after all Paul has suffered from them, take note of the feelings toward them expressed in this closing portion. What can be learned from the attitudes Paul expresses here even after having to write as he has done?

---

[22] Grk *chairo* is to rejoice or be glad, but as often it is used as a greeting upon meeting people (Matt. 26:49; 27:29; Mark 15:18; Luke 1:28; John 19:3) or at the beginning of a letter (Acts 15:23; 23:26; Jas. 1:1), it is sometimes understood here as a closing greeting (farewell, goodbye). See AG, 873 & GT, 663.

Be perfected is from the Greek *katartizo*, akin to *katartisis* in 9b: "*put in order, restore—a. restore to its former condition, put to rights ... ti something* nets (by cleaning, mending, folding together) Mt 4:21; Mk 1:19. ... Pass. *katartizesthe mend your ways* 2 Cor 13:11. b. *put into proper condition, complete, make complete*" (AG, 417b). Paul would pray for their perfecting (9b), but their cooperation was required (11). They must yield to the working of God, the passive indicating: Be put in order, mended, put in the right condition.

Be comforted. Grk *parakaleo* involves the use of speech with a wide range of applications, including urging, exhorting, pleading, encouraging, etc. (See AG, 617 & GT, 482.) Considering the way the epistle began (1:3–7), perhaps Paul is calling upon the Corinthians to let the message of the epistle have its effect; to receive his appeal, admonition and encouragement.

Be of the same mind; be at peace. Closely related exhortations, urging a condition of harmony, as opposed to the dispositions listed in 12:20.

Order Books & Tapes Directly from L. A. Mott

Telephone: 904/744–5624
E-mail: lamott@earthlink.net
Postal Mail: L. A. Mott, Jr., 5361 Timberline Drive, Jacksonville, FL 32277
If you have trouble reaching me, check **www.sunesispublishing.com** for the most up-to-date contact information.

If you would like to order by mail, simply clip this order form, write in the blanks the quantity of each item you wish to order, figure the total on the back, fill in the address blank at the bottom, and send to the postal address above. Your satisfaction is always guaranteed.

Thinking Through the Bible Series

A set of study guides filled with thought-provoking questions and insightful exposition aimed at guiding the diligent student through the thought processes of the Bible's writers. Cassette recordings of class lectures are also available. The careful analysis and probing questions are consistent throughout the series, but the length of exposition varies. The books have a comb binding (except for *Thinking Through Philippians*, which is perfect bound, and *Thinking Through Second Corinthians,* which has a special "lay-flat" binding, called *Otabind*).

___ ***Wisdom and Poetry*** (88 pp.) $8
  ___ Lessons on Cassette $50

___ ***Thinking Through John*** (160 pp.) $12
  ___ Lessons on Cassette $50

___ ***Acts*** (119 pp.) $10
  ___ Lessons on Cassette $45

___ ***Paul's Gospel Among the Gentiles*** (51 pp.) $6.50
  (on the epistle to the Romans)
  ___ Lessons on Cassette $25

___ ***Thinking Through Second Corinthians*** $11.95
  ___ Lessons on Cassette $25

___ ***Thinking Through Philippians*** (123 pp.) $8.95
  a complete exposition of Paul's epistle, without study questions

___ ***Hebrews & James*** (56 pp.) $6.50
  ___ Lessons on Cassette $25

___ **Entire series to date**—25% off

___ **All Tape Sets**—25% off

Name _____

Address _____

City_____ State_____ Zip _____

Telephone _____

E-Mail _____

For more information, including discounts for quantity purchases, contact me or see www.sunesispublishing.com

Study Guides and Tape Recorded Courses on the Books of the Bible

___ Genesis $1.25
  ___ *Lessons on Cassette* ($25)
___ Exodus & Leviticus $3.15
  ___ *Lessons on Cassette* ($25)
___ Numbers/Deuteronomy $2.80
  ___ *Lessons on Cassette* ($25)
___ Joshua–Ruth $1.50
  ___ *Lessons on Cassette* ($25)
___ United Kingdom $2.00
  ___ *Lessons on Cassette* ($50)
___ Divided Kingdom $1.60
  ___ *Lessons on Cassette* ($25)
___ Preexilic Minor Prophets $1.60
  ___ *Lessons on Cassette* ($25)
___ Exile and Return $2.25
  ___ *Lessons on Cassette* ($50)
___ Matthew (tape set only) $50
___ Mark $1.25
  ___ *Lessons on Cassette* ($25)
___ Luke $1.75
  ___ *Lessons on Cassette* ($50)
___ First Cor. $3.50
  ___ *Lessons on Cassette* ($25)
___ Second Cor/Gal $2.00
  ___ *Lessons on Cassette* ($25)
___ Eph.–Col. $1.25
  ___ *Lessons on Cassette* ($25)
___ First Thess.—Philemon $3.00
  ___ *Lessons on Cassette* ($25)
___ First Peter–Jude $4.00
  ___ *Lessons on Cassette* ($25)
___ Revelation $1.65
  ___ *Lessons on Cassette* ($25)
___ All 15 Study Guides ($21.75)

Monographs on Vital Bible Themes (8-16 pages each)

One free; a dozen for $7.50; 25–99, 50 cents each; 100 for $35. Titles may be mixed.

___ 1. The Resurrection of Jesus Christ (the evidence of John)
___ 2. The First Day Meeting at Troas (Acts 20:7 and the Lord's supper)
___ 3. Reading Revelation (basic approach to the book of Revelation)
___ 4. Song of Solomon (complete analysis)
___ 5. Redemption in Christ Jesus (death of Christ: table talks on Romans)
___ 6. The Sinner's Prayer: Calling on the Name of the Lord
___ 7. Wives and Husbands (exposition of Ephesians 5:22–33)
___ 8. Paul Before Agrippa: The Case for Christianity
___ 9. Which Thief on the Cross? (answer to rebuttal on baptism)
___ 10. The Good News for Business People (Conversion of Lydia)
___ 11. Glorying in the Cross (death of Christ: table talks from Galatians)
___ 12. The Great Commission (complete analysis of Matthew 28:18–20)
___ 13. Born From Above (discussion of John 3:5 in context)
___ 14. The Deity of Jesus Christ (emphasis on John 1:1-3)
___ 15. The Ministry of Reconciliation (exposition of 2 Cor. 5:11–6:2)
___ 16. Messiah on Trial (the temptation of Jesus)
___ 17. The Collection for the Saints (exposition of 2 Cor. 8 & 9)

Total Price_____ + 10% s/h _____ + 7.5% tax _____ =
               minimum of $3.50   Florida Residents Only
Total of Order _____ (monographs min. $1)